BITCOIN
FOR TRADERS

Harvey Walsh

shelfless

Bitcoin For Traders

First Published 2018 by Shelfless

First Edition [P1.00]

ISBN 978-1718893023

Shelfless Ltd, Leigh-on-Sea, SS9 2AB, UK

WWW.SHELFLESS.CO.UK

Copyright © Harvey Walsh, 2018

The right of Harvey Walsh to be identified as author of this work has been asserted in accordance with sections 77 and 78 of the Copyright, Designs and Patents Act, 1988.

You may not copy, store, distribute, transmit, reproduce or otherwise make available this publication (or any part of it) in any form, or by any means (electronic, digital, optical, mechanical, photocopying, recording or otherwise), without the prior written permission of the publisher. Any person who does any unauthorised act in relation to this publication may be liable to criminal prosecution and civil claims for damages.

LIMIT OF LIABILITY / DISCLAIMER OF WARRANTY: THE PUBLISHER AND THE AUTHOR MAKE NO REPRESENTATIONS OR WARRANTIES WITH RESPECT TO THE ACCURACY OR COMPLETENESS OF THE CONTENTS OF THIS WORK AND SPECIFICALLY DISCLAIM ALL WARRANTIES, INCLUDING WITHOUT LIMITATION WARRANTIES OF FITNESS FOR A PARTICULAR PURPOSE. NO WARRANTY MAY BE CREATED OR EXTENDED BY SALES OR PROMOTIONAL MATERIALS. THE ADVICE AND STRATEGIES CONTAINED HEREIN MAY NOT BE SUITABLE FOR EVERY SITUATION. THIS WORK IS SOLD WITH THE UNDERSTANDING THAT THE PUBLISHER IS NOT ENGAGED IN RENDERING LEGAL, ACCOUNTING, FINANCIAL, INVESTMENT, OR OTHER PROFESSIONAL SERVICES. IF PROFESSIONAL ASSISTANCE IS REQUIRED, THE SERVICES OF A COMPETENT PROFESSIONAL PERSON SHOULD BE SOUGHT. NEITHER THE PUBLISHER NOR THE AUTHOR SHALL BE LIABLE FOR DAMAGES ARISING HERE FROM. THE FACT THAT AN ORGANISATION OR WEBSITE IS REFERRED TO IN THIS WORK AS A CITATION OR POTENTIAL SOURCE OF FURTHER INFORMATION DOES NOT MEAN THAT THE AUTHOR OR PUBLISHER ENDORSES THE INFORMATION THAT THE ORGANISATION OR WEBSITE MAY PROVIDE OR RECOMMENDATIONS IT MAY MAKE. FURTHERMORE, READERS SHOULD BE AWARE THAT INTERNET WEBSITES LISTED IN THIS WORK MAY HAVE CHANGED OR DISAPPEARED BETWEEN WHEN THIS WORK WAS WRITTEN AND WHEN IT IS READ.

Also By Harvey Walsh

Brain Hacks For Traders

How To Day Trade Forex For Profit

How To Day Trade Stocks For Profit

Available from all good book stores.

Contents

Introduction	1
What Is Bitcoin?	5
What Is Cryptocurrency?	15
Bitcoin Is Different	19
How It Works	25
Why Bitcoin?	51
Why Not Bitcoin?	55
Wallets	65
Exchanges	89
Coins & Symbols	95
Getting Started	99
Trading Opportunities	101
Conventional Trading	103
Unconventional Trading	121
Beware The Pump & Dump	135
Bitcoin As A Useful Currency	139
Final Thoughts	143
Appendix I - Technical Analysis Primer	145
Appendix II - Sample Strategies	169
Glossary	189

Disclaimers

Here are some disclaimers; they look boring, and they are. But they're really important, so please read this page fully.

Here's the TL;DR version: Do your own research. Don't trade with money you can't afford to lose. If you lose money or break the law, it's on you.

Risk Disclosure Statement

All trading carries risk. Trading with cryptocurrencies like Bitcoin carries even more risk. For reasons you will learn in this book, there are more ways to lose money trading cryptocurrencies than almost any other form of trading.

Trading has large potential rewards, and also large potential risk. You must be aware of the risks and be willing to accept them in order to invest in financial markets, including cryptocurrency markets. Do not trade with money that you cannot afford to lose. The contents of this book is for general information purposes only. Although every attempt has been made to assure accuracy, we assume no responsibility for errors or omissions. Examples are provided for illustrative purposes and should not be construed as investment advice or strategy. Hypothetical or simulated performance results have certain inherent limitations; unlike an actual performance record, simulated results do not represent actual trading. Also, since the trades have not actually been executed, the results may have under or over compensated for the impact, if any, of certain market factors, such as lack of liquidity. Past performance is not indicative of future results.

Legality

Bitcoin (and other cryptocurrencies) is regulated in some countries and states, and banned altogether in others. As laws can and do change, it is up to the reader to perform their own due diligence about the legality of cryptocurrency in their country of residence.

The author and publisher accept no responsibility for any losses, financial or otherwise, that may arise from following the methods in this book.

Introduction

Unless you've been living under a rock, or in a remote monastery somewhere, the chances are high you already know something of Bitcoin. It's why you bought this book, after all. Yet for all the publicity the currency has received, especially since its meteoric rise in price in 2017, it remains poorly understood. Misconceptions abound. Like so much to do with new technology and the internet, Bitcoin is one of those things people think they 'sort of get', but the details of which elude them.

The aim of this book is to first demystify what is, at its heart, just another form of value exchange. I'll demonstrate why Bitcoin is actually very simple to understand, even if the technology that makes it work is pretty mind-blowing. And then I'll show you how you, as a trader, can leverage this new kind of money to make profits. We'll look at standard trading techniques and how they can be adapted for this world of digital money, then some not-so-standard ones unique to Bitcoin and other cryptocurrencies. Because Bitcoin itself is not unique.

There are dozens of electronic currencies (often referred to as altcoins, coins, cryptos, or digital tokens) based on the same or similar technologies underpinning Bitcoin. So almost everything in this book also applies to those currencies, like Ethereum, Litecoin, or Monero.

We will cover how to get your money into and out of the Bitcoin ecosystem, how to keep your investments safe from theft or accidental loss (two pitfalls that are magnified in the world of cryptocurrency), and we'll have a look at the other risks associated with Bitcoin — hazards that can catch out the unwary or uninitiated. But don't worry, we'll see how those risks are easily mitigated.

Cryptocurrency is a fast evolving field of technology, but it's here to stay. Maybe Bitcoin itself won't go the distance, but if it fades into obscurity one day, something similar — better, even — will probably take its place. And you will be in the best possible position to profit, whatever happens.

Prerequisites

This book was written by a trader, for traders. It assumes the reader has an understanding of trading concepts and terminology, and has an arsenal of profitable strategies they already use. However, if you are completely new to trading, Appendix 1 covers the bare minimum required to understand the rest of this book, and Appendix 2 offers some basic strategies to kick start your trading adventure.

How To Use This Book

There is logic to the way this volume has been structured. I urge you to try to avoid skipping chapters even if you're familiar with Bitcoin or other cryptocurrencies. Missing out sections may cause confusion later when I refer back to something I covered earlier. Even if you understand the concepts and are reading this for some market specifics, going over the initial chapters is good revision and will remind you why things work the way they do.

Finally, in the text you will see some words are in *italics* when they are first introduced. You can find definitions for these terms in the Glossary at the end of the book.

Bitcoin Or bitcoin?

Throughout this book I use the relatively standard convention of referring to the Bitcoin protocol, network, and ecosystem as Bitcoin (with a capital B), and to the currency unit as bitcoin (with a lowercase b).

What Is Bitcoin?

It a nutshell, Bitcoin is a system of digital money that is not administered by any central authority. Sounds simple, and in a way it is. But before we go any further, we need to unpack that basic definition and make sure we truly understand what Bitcoin is and how it works. Whilst it is possible to profit from Bitcoin — and other cryptocurrencies — without this understanding, we will be doing so at a massive disadvantage to those with a deeper knowledge. A racing car driver who takes the time to find out about how the engine of their vehicle functions, how the suspension works, and how the aerodynamics and tyres help it stick to the track, will outperform a similarly skilled driver who displays little interest in their machinery, because that knowledge will enable them to get the very best out of their equipment. In my years teaching traders, I've seen time and again those who educate themselves on the mechanics of the market regularly outperform those who skip the theory. This is even more true when it comes to Bitcoin because some of the trading opportunities the currency affords derive from its mechanics. Not only that, all the risks associated with Bitcoin are directly linked to the way it works, too. In other words, knowing how Bitcoin functions is the very basis of knowing how to profit from it safely.

Bitcoin is a *cryptocurrency*. In fact, it was the first decentralised cryptocurrency (though not the first cryptocurrency — there were predecessors that whilst less innovative, nonetheless paved the way for Bitcoin). Invented by an anonymous computer programmer or group known only as Satoshi Nakamoto (real identity still unknown at the time of writing) and released as open source software in 2009, Bitcoin was initially slow to take off, due in no small part to the fact that cryptocurrency can be tough to explain. But don't let that put you off. You wouldn't have picked up this book if you weren't keen to know more, and that desire will stand you in good stead. Actually, Bitcoin isn't that hard to understand at all, if you start from the right place. And that place is having a firm grasp of currency as we know it.

What Is Currency?

The Oxford English Dictionary says currency is *"A system of money in general use in a particular country"*. Bitcoin, as we can see, already bends this definition, because it has no respect for national borders. It is truly a global form of money.

Okay, so what is money? That might seem like a silly question. We've all been familiar with money for as long as we've understood that we have to pay for things. But let's break it down, because it's important to understand the mechanics of money to understand how Bitcoin fulfils the same function without any of the infrastructure associated with money as we know it.

In the simplest terms, money is a system of tokens that can be exchanged for goods and services within their scope of acceptance. The tokens can be anything. Most of us are familiar with the tokens we call dollars, pounds, euros, yen, shekels, and so on. The scope of acceptance for those tokens is, as the dictionary reminds us, generally associated with a particular country. Strictly speaking some currencies have greatly increased scopes of acceptance; the US dollar for example, is accepted in many countries because of its relative stability compared to local currencies. The Euro is the national currency of nineteen countries, and it's accepted in quite a few more besides because, like the

US dollar, it is stable and abundant. In other words, demand for these currencies allows them to transcend their original scope of acceptance.

Other tokens may have smaller scopes of acceptance. For example, if you have ever played the online game Second Life, you might be familiar with tokens called Linden Dollars. The scope of those tokens is limited to the virtual world of the game. In some parts of the real world, stones[1], shells[2], and even cheese[3] are used as tokens for commerce.

Ultimately it doesn't matter what the token is called, or what form it takes. As long as everyone who wants to use it is in agreement that the token has *value*, then it is effectively a currency.

Value is an important concept. Really important.

For a token to work as money, there must be general agreement about its value. Once upon a time, value was easy to determine because currency was naturally scarce. Imagine for a moment that you step into a train carriage for a three-hour journey. If the carriage is empty, the value of the seats to you will be determined by their placement and relative comfort. A plush seat with extra legroom, armrests, and perhaps next to a window, will be more prized than a torn scruffy seat beside the toilet. But if the carriage is full to overflowing, and that scruffy seat is the last one left, its value to the passengers competing for it will increase enormously due to its scarcity. Everyone can agree on the value of the seat.

---

[1] - Large round stones called Rai Stones are used as currency on the Island of Yap in Micronesia.

[2] - In Langa Langa lagoon in the Solomon Islands, shells have been used as currency for more than three thousand years, and are still in use today.

[3] - In Emilia Romagna in Italy, Parmigiano Reggiano cheese is accepted as collateral for loans.

Back in the days of the Roman Empire, gold, silver, bronze and copper pieces were the money tokens. These precious metals had to be mined, refined, and worked into coins, a process that consumed a great deal of time, physical effort, and a limited resource. The supply of coins was restricted by the time, effort, and materials available. Scarcity and this finite supply meant value was easy to determine and easy to agree upon.

Eventually gold and silver gave way to commodity metals and paper for money tokens (more recently, cotton, plastic, and composite materials have been used in the manufacture of 'paper' money due to their increased durability). These new tokens abstracted away the value of money from its physical incarnation. But they were still linked back to reserves of precious metals held in bank vaults. The materials used in the coins and bills were worth a fraction of the value they represented — they were tokens in the true sense of the word. Yet because of that connection to real, solid, genuine gold, their value was never in dispute. In effect, they became *I Owe You* notes. Indeed if you read the small print on a British bank note, you will find it says "I promise to pay the bearer on demand the sum of ten pounds" (or whatever the value of the note is). It used to be possible to walk into the Bank of England and enforce this promise; hand over a five pound note to the cashier and, making good on that written promise, they would give you five gold sovereigns in exchange.

So far so good. But there's an inevitable problem with this system of money. Linking a money token to a physical object like gold means you are limiting the quantity of tokens that can exist. There is a finite supply of gold in the world. More can be mined, but one day it will run out (unless we get into mining asteroids, but that's nitpicking).

One way around this limitation is to reduce the amount of gold a money token represents. If, for example, one US dollar is worth one thirty-fifth of a troy ounce of gold, as was the case in 1971, then a solution to the supply problem could be to change that value to one seventieth of a troy ounce. You've doubled the potential money pool at a stroke. But really this is just kicking the can down the road. Pull that trick enough times, and sooner or later the amount of gold a dollar is worth will become so small as to be immeasurable — and worthless. So in reality, linking the value of money to gold places a ceiling on the amount of money that can reasonably exist. If a government wants their economy to grow — and what government doesn't? — then a limit on the money supply is a problem.

Recognising this fact, in 1971 President Nixon 'nixxed' the link between the US dollar and gold. Actually that process had already begun after the end of the Second World War, Nixon only broke the final link. One day thirty-five dollars was worth a troy ounce of gold, the next it was worth, well, thirty-five dollars. To the man and woman on the street, nothing had visibly changed. The removal of the so-called gold standard was a technical exercise that didn't concern them, which is why money continued to work. The dollar continued to have value because everyone believed it had value.

Currencies like the US dollar, that have value only because the issuing body (a government or national reserve or central bank) says they do, are called *fiat* currencies.

If you're thinking, *"Hang on, fiat money sounds like it's a global scam,"* then you are right. Sort of. Money is a confidence trick, an illusion. Except we are all willing participants in the trick. We have all chosen to go along with it. As long as we collectively believe that our money can be exchanged for goods and services indefinitely, that money continues to have value.

Naturally, not everyone will have the same idea of what the value is. This is great news for readers of this book because differing opinions on the value of currency (or indeed any commodity or stock) are what give us traders the opportunity to trade it and profit from it.

For a nation, fiat currency allows the economy to grow without limit. To see how an economy can grow, we need to understand where new money comes from.

Where Does Money Come From?

Glad you asked. In the case of fiat currencies like the dollar, pound, or euro, new money can come into existence in two ways. In a normal, functioning, growing economy, most money is created from debt. When a commercial bank (that's the sort you find on the high street, rather than a central bank like the Bank of England) lends money, you might imagine it owns the money it is lending. Seems a reasonable expectation, but it's not the case. Banks work on a reserve system, which means that they are only required to hang on to a fraction of their customers' deposits. The rest of those deposits can be lent out as loans. This is called *fractional reserve banking*. The exact fraction of deposits a bank must retain is fixed by the appropriate regulatory body — again this may be a government or a central bank. The US and the UK have slightly differing systems, the US has a reserve requirement and the UK and some other countries have a capital requirement, but for the purposes of our high-level overview, these perform the same function in that they limit how much money a commercial bank can lend.

An example will make things easier to understand. For the sake of simplicity, let's say that a state has a fractional reserve requirement of ten percent, which is roughly the actual figure in most large economies. That means if you go and put $100,000 into your bank account, your bank is only required to hang on to $10,000 of the money. They are free to lend out the other $90,000 to their customers.

At this point you may be thinking, *"What if I want my money back?"* Reasonable question. The answer is simple. The bank will give you your money whenever you want it. They don't have to go out and call in their loans in order to repay you because in reality the money they lent out was new money. Of course, the bank didn't go and physically print $90,000 worth of bills to be able to lend it. Most money in the world is not held in physical coins or bills, but in lines on a ledger. When another customer walked into the bank and asked for a $90,000 loan to buy a very nice car, contrary to what we might like to imagine, the banker did not walk into the safe, count out $90,000 in cash, and deposit it into the customer's own Gringotts-esque[4] private vault. What really happens is the transaction is recorded in a big database, like a kind of giant spreadsheet, that keeps track of who has what in their account. The transfer of funds is simply recorded as a ledger entry. The money is all virtual.

What all of this means is that you still have access to your $100,000 whenever you want it, and the customer who took out the loan now has $90,000 in their account. That's money that didn't exist anywhere in the world before. The bank plucked the money out of thin air and made it 'real'. The economy just grew a little bit. Your original $100,000 has almost doubled!

But it goes much further than that. At some point the person who took out the loan takes their $90,000 and buys that car with it. The vendor selling the car takes the money and deposits it into their bank account. Their bank's capital has grown by $90,000, and they only have to hang on to 10% of it, or $9,000. They can lend out the other $81,000.

---

4 - Gringotts is the fictional Goblin-run bank from the Harry Potter series of books and films.

So now our original $100,000 has grown to $100,000 + $90,000 + $81,000 = $271,000.

When that $81,000 is loaned out, spent, and deposited, 90% of it can be loaned out too, and so on. In fact, with a 10% reserve, every dollar initially introduced into the system can eventually grow to $10. Our original $100,000 deposit can grow to a million dollars.

Of course, over time all those loans will slowly be paid back and all that new money will cease to exist; it will evaporate back into the air. For every ten dollars paid back, the bank will effectively be keeping one and erasing nine from the world. But as long as new loans are being created, the economy grows[5].

Now we understand that money comes from debt, we can see why decreases in consumer spending are disastrous for the economy. We are often taught that debt is bad, and on an individual level I'd agree — eradicating debt from your life is generally the best investment you can make. But on a national and international level, debt is not only essential to the economy, it basically *is* the economy.

If this is making your head spin, don't worry, it's a mind-bending concept. The takeaway here is that new money comes from the creation of debt; it's made literally out of thin air. A few keystrokes on a computer, or more likely a computer program automatically accepting a loan application, is all it takes to make new money appear.

Debt accounts for most new money that comes into the world (estimates vary, but we can safely assume that more than 80% of money is created from debt), but it's not the only way. The second path by which new money comes into existence is again, to create it out of thin air. This time it's the state that does the money creation, via a nation-

---

5 - And if you think that makes the entire economy basically a giant Ponzi scheme, I'd tend to agree!

al reserve or central bank. You might have heard about this process on the news; sometimes it is euphemistically called quantitive easing. Often it's simply referred to as printing money. In reality little or no money is physically printed in a mint, the money is created by making an entry on a ledger in a central bank, who then lends it to commercial banks to increase their deposits and so the amount debt (i.e. money) they can create. Sounds great, right? Who wouldn't want to print more money? There is a catch, of course. Adding more money in this way dilutes the value of all the money in the system, which can cause deflation. Less money being spent makes for a shrinking economy, so quantitive easing can backfire. It's something economists love to argue about.

Summary

This has been a very simplistic overview of currency, but there are some key points I want you to take away before we move on to see how cryptocurrencies like Bitcoin fit into the economy.

- Regular so-called fiat currencies like dollars and pounds and euros, are a system of tokens, accepted by the masses as a satisfactory means of enabling commerce.

- Fiat currency has no intrinsic value, it is worth only what those using it agree it is worth.

- Differing opinions on the current and projected value of fiat currencies provide opportunities for traders to make profits.

- Because fiat currency has no intrinsic value, its supply is limited only by regulation.

- New fiat money can enter the economy either as new debt, or by being created by the currency-issuing body.

- I've alluded to this throughout this section, but let's make it clear: fiat currencies are regulated either by governments or a national reserve or central bank. It is they who ultimately control the supply of fiat money by regulating debt creation and by printing new money.

Now we have an understanding of regular money, let's move on and see how cryptocurrency breaks some of the rules, and in one way could even be considered a step backwards.

What Is Cryptocurrency?

Cryptocurrency can be thought of most simplistically as digital money with no central governing authority. The 'crypto' part of the name comes from the way the currency works on a technical level, using cryptography (secret codes, if you like) to make it secure and unforgeable.

In some ways, cryptocurrencies like Bitcoin and Monero aren't that different to regular currencies. In fact, Bitcoin is closer to the money of old because like gold, there is a finite supply of bitcoins as we will see later. This scarcity alone gives bitcoin implicit value.

Like other fiat currencies, bitcoin and its ilk also derive value from the agreement of the masses. And as always, there are variations in what the masses think about its value — cue trading opportunities! But more on those later.

The real differences between cryptocurrency and the money in your pocket come from how it is created, and how it is transferred from one person to another. To understand that, let's look a little closer at the first and best known cryptocurrency, Bitcoin. This is an overview — we'll dig deeper later on.

What Is A Bitcoin?

When you own ten dollars, or ten pounds, or ten euros, you either own physical tokens (coins or bills) representing that money, or you have it in some form of account from which you can withdraw it as tokens. Either way, your money can be made manifest more or less at will.

When you own a bitcoin, there is no token. You cannot withdraw your bitcoin from a bank in the form of an actual coin, or a bitcoin bill, there's no such thing. What you own is *control* over that bitcoin — an ability to spend it.

Bitcoin is stored in a *wallet* (lots more on wallets later), which for now we can think of as being a bit like a bank account, just without the bank. At its simplest, a wallet comprises two things:

- An address (analogous to an email address)
- A secret code that controls the address (like a password controlling access to an email address)

To spend bitcoin, you send it to someone else's address using your secret code to authorise the transaction. That bitcoin is subsequently under the other person's control.

So far, so normal. Sounds similar to a wire transfer from a bank account, right? If I transferred money from my account to yours, and we were at the same bank, the transaction would be recorded in the bank's ledger. Because we all trust the banks, we all agree on their version of events when they tell us that the money is now in your account and not mine. If your account was at a different bank to mine, our two banks would collaborate and update their ledgers accordingly, and we'd all still be in agreement about where the money was.

With Bitcoin, there is no bank, so how do we keep track of the transaction? If I send you a bitcoin, how would you know that you had received it?

The answer lies in a rather special ledger, called a *blockchain*. This ledger isn't managed by or held at a bank, it's held publicly by lots and lots of people. Even you or I can hold a copy of it if we want (and if we have the space on our hard drives — it's pretty big!)

When a bitcoin transfer is initiated, details of it are sent out to the internet to anyone who has a copy of the blockchain ledger. Those details include the address of the wallet sending the funds, the address those funds are going to, and the amount being sent. Through a process called *mining*, which we will examine later, the transaction's details are indelibly written into every one of the thousands of copies of the decentralised blockchain ledger. Because of some clever maths and economics, effectively nobody can ever modify the transaction once it has been written, it's there forever. Because everyone has access to the blockchain, everyone can see that the transaction occurred and everyone agrees that I no longer own the funds and you do.

So in essence, there is no such thing as *a* bitcoin, there is only a trace of where a bitcoin has been spent. Sure, you can look at a wallet and it will give you a figure for how many bitcoins are in there, but that figure is derived from the entire history of transactions. There isn't actually anything in the wallet at all. Mind-bending, right? But if you think about it, regular money works the same way — if you ignore cash.

Bitcoin Is Different

Cryptocurrencies like Bitcoin are both familiar and different to the kind of currency we've all grown up with. Let's have a look at some of the most important ways how.

Transparency

Your bank account is your business. Your transaction history is between you and your bank. I can't see where you've been spending your hard-earned money. Your bank can, though, and so can the government and law enforcement, provided they have a warrant.

Bitcoin is often hyped in the media as being an anonymous and untraceable currency, and this has earned it a reputation as the currency of choice among criminals and buyers of drugs and arms. But this reputation is based on a lack of understanding about how Bitcoin works. The reality is somewhat different.

The blockchain ledger in which every Bitcoin transaction is written, is entirely open and transparent. If I send you some bitcoin, I can look at the blockchain and see it arrive in your wallet. And if you use the same address to spend that bitcoin subsequently, I can keep looking and see the address you send it to. This isn't some special access granted to me because I sent you the bitcoin in the first place — anyone else in the world with an internet connection can also look at the blockchain ledger and see your transactions.

However, the blockchain ledger only lays bare wallet addresses. A wallet address is a long sequence of digits (about thirty, it's not fixed) which has no relation to your name, indeed no identifying features at all. No bank issues these addresses, we can generate them ourselves. If I don't know your wallet address, I can't look at its activity. The same goes for the government and the police, which is why Bitcoin gets its reputation for anonymity. Even if I did know your address, I'd be unlikely to recognise the addresses you were spending your bitcoin at. Looking through the blockchain ledger at your transaction history would be like looking at your recent call history on your phone — I'd see a lot of numbers, but without names attached they would mean nothing to me.

So Bitcoin can offer some anonymity through the obscurity of wallet addresses. Just how much depends on how the currency is used. It is sometimes said that Bitcoin is anonymous until you spend it, and that's because at the time you spend it you will probably be divulging some personal details. For example, if you order something online to be mailed to you, you will need to include your name and mailing address for the delivery. The merchant you buy from can link the Bitcoin address you pay with, to your name. And if you decide to *cash out* — to sell your bitcoin for a fiat currency like dollars — the currency exchange at which you perform this transaction will probably have verified your identity beforehand. They too will be able to link your address to your name. A police warrant can oblige them to hand over that information.

If you always use the same address when you receive and spend bitcoin, it will be easy for anyone to follow your transactions using a service like blockchain.info. But if you mix it up and never reuse an address, which is easy enough to do, your spending habits will be somewhat lost in a sea of indecipherable numbers. Bear in mind though, that sooner or later, if you use bitcoin to pay for anything, the chances are you will be creating a link between your transactions and your identity. Bitcoin is transparent, it is not anonymous.

24/7

Banks have people working in them. People sleep occasionally, and take vacations, so banks tend to close at night and weekends. Sure, we have on-line banking now, but there are still 'banking hours'. Send a wire transfer on a Sunday and it more often than not won't actually happen until Monday. Or Tuesday, if Monday happens to be a bank holiday, because they're a thing too. Send bitcoin on Sunday and it will go there and then[6]. Bitcoin never sleeps.

Unregulated

Bitcoin is, by and large, unregulated. Please note that this is not the case everywhere in the world. Some countries have introduced laws restricting its use, and others have banned the currency altogether. Laws change, and it is up to you the reader to check on the legality of cryptocurrencies in your country of residence before embarking on any kind of trading. Disclaimer out of the way, what does a lack or regulation mean for Bitcoin in practice? Imagine if our dollars, pounds, and euros were handled only in cash. That's how Bitcoin works.

If you pay someone for something with cash, and give them too much money, it's up to them to give you back the overpayment. Without a bank involved in the process, you have no recourse to a higher authority. It's entirely down to the goodwill of the receiving party to correct the error. That's how Bitcoin works, too.

If you saw an ad for something on eBay and sent the seller an envelope stuffed with cash, but messed up the mailing address and sent it to the wrong person, that cash would

---

6 - There are some caveats to this, to do with fees, discussed later in this book.

be lost. The receiving party *might* make the effort to trace the source of their unexpected windfall and send it back, but realistically? The money is gone. That's how Bitcoin works, too.

If you did get the address right, but the seller decided to do a bunk with your envelope full of cash and not send you the goods, you'd be out of pocket. You wouldn't have any bank guarantee or Paypal protection to fall back on. That's how Bitcoin works, too.

No bank running the show means there's no oversight and nobody to run to if things go wrong with a Bitcoin transaction. If you have trouble sending money from your bank account, your bank's customer service team will be there to advise. Have the same problem with Bitcoin, and you *might* get help from whoever made your wallet if you're using a software wallet, but by and large you are on your own.

Moreover, if you make a mistake, it's on you. The only person in the world who can send bitcoin is the person (or persons) who have the secret key to the wallet it is stored in. There is no controlling authority who can step in and right a wrong.

If someone gets hold of the keys to your house, sneaks in at night, and takes all your cash, that money is lost. That's how Bitcoin works, too. If someone gets hold of your secret key and uses it to send the contents of your wallet to theirs, your money is gone.

If you keep your money in a bank, you have guarantees. In most countries, commercial bank accounts have protection offered by central banks or the state. If a bank collapses, your money (up to the limit of the guarantee), is protected. If your credit or debit card is stolen, your losses are limited by the issuing bank's guarantees. The same cannot be said for Bitcoin.

A final note on the unregulated nature of Bitcoin. In most developed countries, commercial banks have a legal requirement to divulge information about their customers to government. They are also legally bound to 'know their customer'. They must ask certain questions about large deposits, satisfy themselves that money coming in has been legally obtained, and report their findings back to whoever collects the taxes. Bitcoin, my earlier disclaimer aside, flies under the radar. No tax authority knows anything about your bitcoin holdings unless you choose to tell them.

Important: I am not advocating tax avoidance or evasion. Please seek the advice of a tax professional qualified in your jurisdiction for all matters regarding your tax liabilities.

Not Legal Tender

Regular currency is legal tender, meaning its use as currency within the issuing country or region is enshrined in law. A shop in the UK cannot refuse Sterling; a restaurant in France must accept remittance in euros; a train company in America is required to take payment in US dollars. All of these people are free to accept other currencies in addition to their native legal tender, but they are not required to do so.

Nobody is legally required to accept bitcoin, or any other cryptocurrency, and it is highly unlikely that they ever will be. So if your favourite fishmonger wakes up one morning and decides that Ethereum is yesterday's hotness and he's going back to good old pounds and pence, you're out of luck if you wanted to settle your bill with that particular payment method.

By the same token, no employer is obliged to pay a salary in bitcoin. No company is legally bound to disburse dividends in a cryptocurrency. No tradesperson can demand payment in Litecoin.

Legal tender will always have some kind of value because the law says it must be accepted as payment for goods and services, and because governments collect and spend taxes in it. Bitcoin has no such status and could become worthless overnight.

How It Works

Now I'm going to have to ask you to bear with me here, because we're going to cover a few concepts, some of which might not make sense immediately. As we go on and look in more detail, these concepts should snap into place and it will all come together.

Side note: You could skip this chapter and get straight to the stuff about trading, but you would be doing yourself a disservice if you do. As I said at the start, the best traders, the most successful, understand their tools and understand what they are working with on a deeper level than the man in the street. You can work with Bitcoin without knowing anything of its internals, and lots of people do, but you will constantly be bombarded with terminology that makes no sense; that can be unsettling at best and terrifying at worst. If there's one thing a trader needs to eliminate from their work, it's fear. This chapter is going to get a tiny bit technical, but only enough to provide sufficient knowledge to have a firm grasp of what's going on when you hit those buy and sell buttons. Moreover, Bitcoin is not like normal money, it is a minefield of risk. There are more ways to lose bitcoin than just about any other store of value. The unregulated cryptocurrency world attracts undesirables of every flavour, eager to separate the uninitiated from their hard earned money. Understanding how Bitcoin works is the best way to make sure you don't get caught out — by a scammer, or by carelessness. Skip this chapter at your own risk!

Cryptography Primer

Bitcoin and its like are cryptocurrencies — currencies secured by cryptography. If we are to get a handle on how they work, we need to know what cryptography is and roughly how it works.

The Oxford English Dictionary defines the word cryptography as *the art of writing or solving codes*, which is a nice concise explanation. Codes have been used for centuries to secure communications from prying eyes. All secret codes use some form of key to lock and unlock messages, a bit like we use passwords now to lock our computers and phones. Traditional codes, like Germany's famous Enigma code used during World War Two, relied on a single key shared between the sender and receiver of the encoded message. The sending party (the high command for example) would use a key to encrypt the message they wanted to transmit, and the receiving party (the divisions on the front line, or the U-boat captains) would use the same key to decrypt it. As long as the enemy didn't get hold of the key, in theory the communication was secure. (In the case of Enigma, a British team including Alan Turing, cracked the code, leading indirectly to the invention of the world's first programmable computer, but that's another story).

Standard cryptography like Enigma can be thought of as a locked box. We put the message we want to hide inside the box and lock it with a key, send the box to the receiving party, and they use a copy of the same key to unlock it and retrieve the message. The problem with this method of communication is that both sending and receiving parties must have a copy of the same key before any dispatch can be sent. When talking about codes rather than locked boxes, the key is a piece of text, like a password, so it's easy to copy. But it can't be transmitted between parties in the open, as the enemy will pick it up too and will be able to use it to decrypt subsequent messages. So in traditional systems like Enigma, the key is shared between sender and receiver long before any encoded transmissions are sent, in person. With Enigma, the key was changed every day in case it fell into enemy hands. The divisions on the battle front, and the U-boat captains, all carried code books listing the keys for the days and weeks ahead. Obviously these books were extremely closely guarded because if the enemy got hold of them, all bets were off.

To get around the problem of having to share keys in advance, modern codes use a system called *public key cryptography*, also called *asymmetric cryptography*. In public key cryptography, the sending and receiving parties use different keys to encode and decode the message (hence asymmetric). Doesn't sound like it should work, right? Thanks to some clever mathematics and some very large prime numbers, it's entirely possible. Don't worry, I dislike mathematics as much as the next man (quite probably more so), but we can understand public key cryptography without so much as adding two numbers together.

To get to grips with the concept, let's return to our analogy of a locked box. We'll imagine that I want to send a message to you securely. You have a box with a lock on it that you give me so I can secure the message inside before sending it back to you. The lock on this box is rather special because unlike most locks, this one has three possible positions. With a key inserted and the lock turned to the 12 o'clock posi-

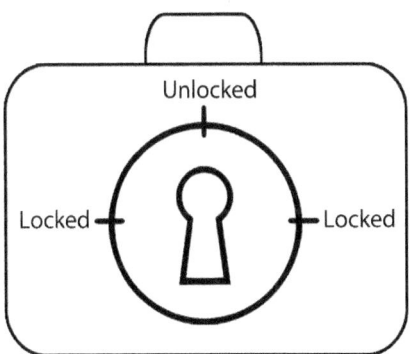

tion, the box is unlocked. If the lock is turned left to the 9 o'clock position, the box is locked. The lock can also be turned right to the 3 o'clock position, which will also lock it.

Here's the clever bit. There are two completely different keys that work this box. One key when inserted into the lock, only turns clockwise. We'll call this the *private key*, for reasons that will become clear. The second key only turns anti-clockwise. That key we will call the *public key*.

You can give out copies of the anti-clockwise turning public key to anyone you like, because as we will see, this key cannot compromise the safety of our communication.

Because I'm going to send a message to you and we don't want anyone else to be able to read it, you first give me a copy of your public key. You don't need to hand it to me in person, you can send it in the mail, or leave one somewhere for me to pick up. It doesn't really matter if anyone else gets hold of the key and makes a copy.

I write out my message, place it into your box with the special lock, then I take the key you sent me and use it to turn the lock from the 12 o'clock position (unlocked) to the 9 o'clock position (locked). Remember, that public key only turns anti-clockwise, so once I've locked the box with it, I can't then unlock it. And neither can anyone else who has a copy of that key. Now we see why it doesn't matter if someone else took a copy of the key while it was in transit.

I send the box to you, safe in the knowledge that if the courier driver, or somebody else en route, finds a copy of your public key (which you're handing out willingly to anyone who asks) they won't be able to open the box with it. That key only goes anti—clockwise.

When you receive the box, you take your private key — the one there are no copies of — and use it to turn the lock clockwise, back to the 12 o'clock unlocked position. Now you can open the box and retrieve my message.

Clever, right? If the German's had used a system like this in the Second World War, they could have done away with the code books containing all the secret keys for the days to come. Instead, the high command could have freely and openly broadcast their public key for the world to hear. It wouldn't matter if the Allies got hold of it, they would only have been able to use it to lock messages (encrypt them), not to unlock (decrypt) them.

But what about that other locked position on the box, the one at 3 o'clock? Let's imagine you wanted to send me a note. You're not worried about keeping the text secret, but I need to be absolutely certain that when I receive it, I am getting the note that was sent from you, not a fake message dispatched by someone else. In this scenario, you write out your message, put it into the box, then you take your private key and turn the lock clockwise from the 12 o'clock unlocked position to the 3 o'clock locked position. You send me the box, and when I get it I take my copy of your public key, and use it to turn the lock anti-clockwise (the only direction my key works in) back to the 12 o'clock unlocked position. If my copy of your key fits the box, then I know the box was from you. If it doesn't fit, someone else must have sent the box, impersonating you. So I can read your message, safe in the knowledge that it definitely came from you.

In public key cryptography, using a private key to secure a message like this is called a *digital signature*, and it is crucial to the way Bitcoin works.

In the above scenario, anyone else with a copy of your public key could open the message too, so the transmission in that direction would not be secure. But if I also had a special box of my own, and I too had a private key and a public key, I could give you my public key, you could put your box inside my box, lock my box with my public key, and send it back to me. Because only I have the private key to open my box, nobody could read or tamper with its contents (which is your box!) So now we have a way of sending a secret message that nobody else can read, *and* that I can be certain has come from you.

In real public key cryptography, there are no magic boxes of course, and no physical keys. The keys we use are actually numbers — very long numbers. Like the keys in the locked box analogy, we use a public and private key pair. The public key is one long number that can be handed out and shared around. It is used to encrypt a message. Mathematically related to it, the private key is another long number that can be used to decrypt a message, or to digitally sign one.

Public key cryptography is what makes secure communications on the internet work. Every time you see that little padlock symbol on a web browser — when you are buying something, or checking your bank account, or even your email these days — you are using public key cryptography. In the background, hidden from view, your bank has sent you its public key, and your web browser has sent your bank your public key. Every subsequent exchange of data — the pages the website sends you, and the credit card numbers you send back, are both encrypted and digitally signed, guaranteeing their provenance and preventing anyone who might be eavesdropping from seeing what's going on.

There's one more thing to understand about public key cryptography. If we think back to our example above, and the message I sent you in the box with the special lock, there is a potential weakness in the system. The courier who takes the box from me to you might, in theory, try to break open the lock with a lock-pick. Or they might try to smash open the box and reverse-engineer the lock, then fabricate their own key to fit it. They *might*, but if the box was strong enough, it would take them so long it wouldn't be worth it.

In the real world, this so-called *brute force* method of attacking encrypted communication is also possible. You could program a computer to generate random private keys (after all, they're just very long numbers), to see if it could find the one that unlocks a message. But if the key number is long enough, it will take a very long time. In fact, the numbers used in modern cryptography are so long that even with the fastest supercomputers in existence, it would take an attacker longer to try every combination than the expected lifespan of our sun. We're talking hundreds of millions of years. The world would quite literally end before the task was accomplished. So unless quantum computers come along and exponentially increase computing power within our lifetimes, we can safely assume that public key cryptography is very, very secure[7].

While the mathematics that make public key encryption possible are fascinating if you like that sort of thing, they are beyond the scope of this book. What we need to take away from this section is this:

> • Public key cryptography uses a very long number called a public key, which can be freely shared, and a mathematically related different long number called a private key, which should never be shared.

---

[7] - Actually any method of cryptography can only ever be *theoretically* secure. Once humans get involved, the potential for errors is introduced and weaknesses can creep in. Mistakes in implementations are one possible weakness. Other so-called attack vectors come from what those in the trade call *side channel attacks* — that is to say, indirect means of attacking communication, such as forcing someone to reveal their private key. The Meltdown and Spectre bugs discovered inside almost every modern computer in 2017 are another example of a side channel attack, as they allow an attacker to read the memory in a computer and discover private keys that way. That said, public key cryptography is the best we've got today, and it's so hard and expensive to break that we can consider it secure.

- The public key can be used to encrypt any kind of information so that it cannot be read.

- The only two ways to decrypt that information are 1) Wait a few hundred million years for the fastest computers on the planet to perform the task (and pay the electricity bill that goes along with that feat), or 2) Use the private key to do it.

- Anyone who has the private key can decrypt the information. So private keys should be kept safe and secure.

- A private key can also be used to digitally sign any piece of information.

- The related public key can then 'unlock' that signature, verifying that it is real and that the information has not been altered or tampered with by a third party.

Great, hopefully we now understand what public and private keys are. We're ready to move on to see how Bitcoin works.

There Is No Bitcoin

The first thing we must understand about Bitcoin is that there is no such thing as *a bitcoin*. Sorry to disappoint you (but I did allude to this earlier). When you own US dollars, or sterling, or euros, you can exchange numbers on a bank balance for physical coins and bills, and vice versa. When someone pays you in one of those currencies, the money goes into an account, or a wallet, or a jam jar, and becomes an integral and indistinguishable part of your balance. Think of it as like a jug of water. If someone added a glass of water to the jug, the water level would increase as a whole. You could not subsequently subtract that exact same glass of water from the jug, only the equivalent amount of water. Unless you deal exclusively in cash, that's how regular money works.

Bitcoin is different. We can't deal exclusively in cash with Bitcoin. Indeed we can't deal in cash at all because there are no physical coins or bills. I cannot send you *a bitcoin*, because there is no such thing as *a bitcoin*. What I can do is send you the *value* of a bitcoin. When I do that, I create a transaction — a ledger entry — that tells the world I have sent you the value of one bitcoin. Because everyone can see the open ledger, the blockchain, that runs the system, everyone is in agreement that my bitcoin balance has been reduced by the value of one bitcoin, and yours has increased by the same value. On the surface that might look indistinguishable from any other kind of currency, but it throws up some interesting mechanical differences that we will need to know about if we are to have a full understanding of how this all works.

The transaction is at the heart of how Bitcoin functions. All Bitcoin really is, is a (very) long list of transactions detailing every transfer of the currency from one owner to the next. We'll see how new bitcoins come into existence later. First, we're going to get into the nuts and bolts of how bitcoin is transacted.

In order to send or receive bitcoin, we need four things:

    1.   A Bitcoin address of our own. For now we can think of this as being like a bank account number (although it's not).

    2.   A private key linked to our address.

    3.   A public key linked to our private key and our address.

    4.   Another Bitcoin address with which we wish to transact.

In practice, the public and private keys are hidden from us, handled by the software we are using to transact. That software is called a *wallet*, and we'll cover wallets in lots more detail later. It's important to understand the role of these keys though.

Now, let's say I want to send you one bitcoin. The first thing I would need is your address. Your address is a number about thirty digits long. It would look something like this:

```
1MtG4xaFyB64ZDCyxY6XUxaSuTpqkD4qTM
```

I enter the address into my wallet software. Because it's hard to type in such a long number without making mistakes, and because any mistake would result in me sending money to the wrong person or to a non-existent address, losing it forever, you might give me a QR code for me to scan with my phone instead. This is the QR code for the above bitcoin address:

Next I tell my wallet how much I want to send you. In this example, one bitcoin. My wallet looks for a bitcoin that I have previously received but have not yet spent. Now, there's a bit of a 'chicken and egg' situation here, so this is where you're going to have to bear with me. All will become clear, I promise.

I said before that there is no such thing as *a bitcoin,* so my wallet can't look for *a bitcoin* to send you. I also said transactions are at the heart of Bitcoin. We can resolve these two statements by thinking of bitcoins as *being* transactions. Let's imagine a transaction as being a little box, like this:

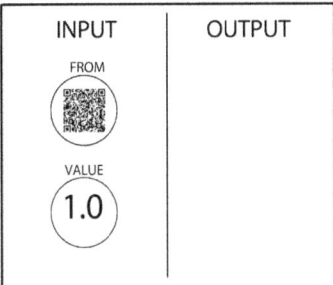

The box is split into two parts, input and output. In the input section, the box contains the address that sent me the transaction originally, and the value of the transaction. If the value of this transaction box was one bitcoin, then the transaction itself is, as far as we are concerned, *a bitcoin.*

Still with me? Good. So my wallet software peeks inside its list of transactions, finds this transaction box I previously received worth one bitcoin, and says *"Great, this is the one I can send out."*

To do that, it fills in the output side of the box by putting your Bitcoin address in there as the destination, my address as the sender, and lops off the input box because you don't need to know about that bit. Now my 'transaction box' looks like this:

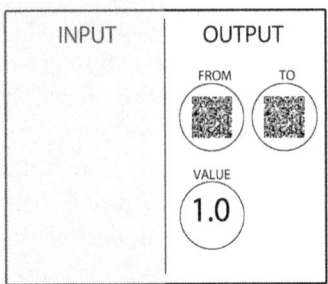

Next my wallet 'locks' the box with my private key linked to my Bitcoin address. If we recall the cryptography primer, we can think of this as me putting my address, your address, and a bitcoin all together into a box and using my private key to turn the lock from the unlocked 12 o'clock position to the locked 3 o'clock position. Then the wallet software sticks my public key to the outside of the transaction. This is like me taping my public key to the top of the locked box. This is what the transaction box looks like now.

Doesn't look very secure, what with the key to unlock the encrypted part being stuck to the outside, does it? That's okay, we're not trying to hide this transaction from anyone. Quite the opposite in fact, because now my wallet is going to broadcast it to the whole Bitcoin network, handing out copies of it to as many people as it can find.

The Bitcoin network is a *peer-to-peer network* comprising all the computers running appropriate software at any given instant in time (such a computer is called a *node*). My wallet software looks on the internet, finds someone who happens to have suitable software running, and sends them a copy of the transaction box. It finds a few more nodes and sends them copies too. Those nodes in turn send out more copies to any nodes *they* can find. In this way, with nodes sending on the transaction to their peers, copies of my transaction spread around the world in a matter of seconds.

Remember, my public key was attached to the transaction, so anyone who gets a copy can use it to unlock it and look inside. Because *only* my public key can open the transaction, and because that public key is indelibly and mathematically linked to my Bitcoin address (which is written down inside the transaction), it means anyone who checks can be 100% certain it was me who sent the transaction, not someone else pretending to be me.

When you next open your wallet software, it starts communicating with any nodes it can find on the internet. It sends out a message saying *"Hey there, what have I missed since I've been away? Anyone got anything for me?"* Nearby nodes will respond, letting it know about any transactions that have your address as a destination. In this way, it will receive a copy of my transaction box. Your wallet will verify my digital signature (by unlocking the box with my attached public key) and conclude that I was indeed the true sender, and will update your balance to show that you now own the bitcoin I sent you. Because everyone who uses Bitcoin can see copies of the transaction, everyone is in agreement that you now own the bitcoin I sent[8].

Inside your wallet, the transaction box now looks like this:

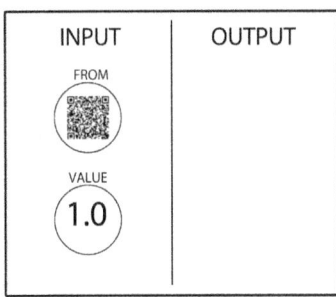

---

8 - There's a bit more to it, but we'll get to that.

What my wallet filled in as an *output* has become an *input* in your wallet. As long as the *output* side of that transaction box remains empty, it means you have not sent it on to anyone else and are therefore the owner.

If you receive other transactions from other Bitcoin users, your wallet might look something like this:

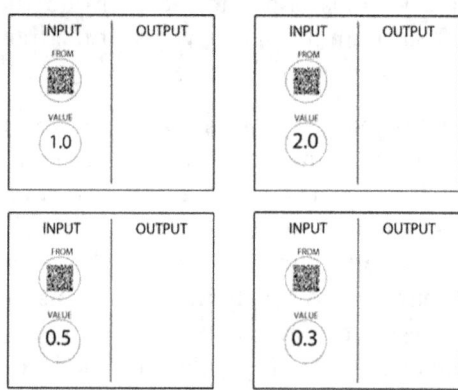

What you have here are four transactions with empty (i.e. unspent) outputs. In Bitcoin terminology these are called *unspent transaction outputs*, or UTXOs for short. For all practical purposes, these UTXOs *are* bitcoins, or fractions of bitcoins. As we can see from the diagram, unlike adding a glass of water to a jug, or depositing some money into a bank account, the UTXOs do not become subsumed into one big blob that makes up the whole. They remain uniquely identified individual transactions. The balance the wallet software shows you is simply the sum of all your UTXOs.

If you want to send a bitcoin to someone, your wallet software will rifle through its UTXOs and find one worth one bitcoin, fill in the output, lop off the input, sign it, and send it out to the network. If you wanted to send 1.3 bitcoins, it would have to use both the UTXO worth 1 bitcoin, *and* the one worth 0.3 bitcoin, filling in the outputs of both and sending them on. Because everyone can see the outputs filled in on the network, everyone agrees where the bitcoin now resides.

What happens though, if you want to send 0.7 bitcoin? A transaction box cannot have its value changed, so you could not send the 1 bitcoin UTXO and keep back 0.3 of its value. Either you send all of that transaction box, or you send none of it.

Fortunately Satoshi Nakamoto considered this when he/she/they came up with the Bitcoin specification. While you cannot subdivide a transaction you have already received and keep a fraction of it in your wallet, you can split it up when you send it out. You do this by creating multiple *outputs*. You put your own Bitcoin address as the second output, and you tell it that you want 0.3 bitcoin-worth of that UTXO to go to your address. Thus your wallet will send 0.7 bitcoin to the destination address, and 0.3 bitcoin right back to itself, creating a brand new unspent transaction output worth 0.3 bitcoin in your wallet. We call this second output *change*. Just to be clear, unlike change from a shop when paying with regular currency, Bitcoin change is always sent by our own wallet back to itself. We don't send the whole amount to the destination address and hope they return the balance. The diagram on the next page shows change in operation.

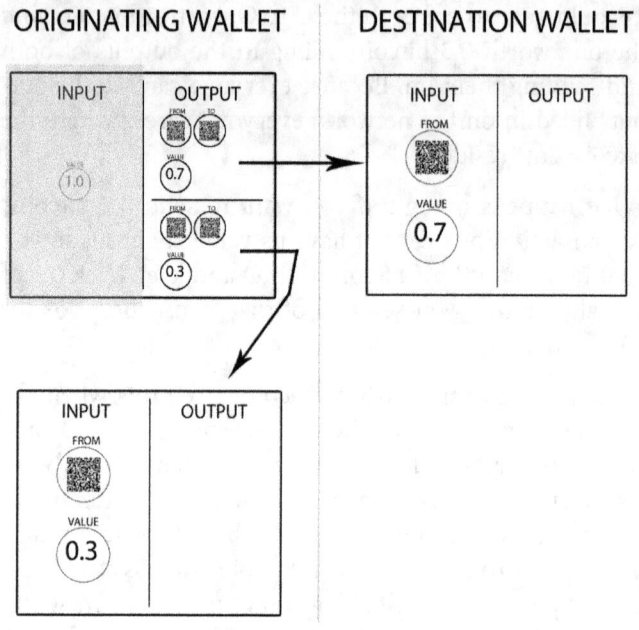

Not Done Yet

We've seen how a transaction is used to transfer value from one party to another, and how everyone who is participating in the Bitcoin network can see every transaction. We've covered how we sign our outgoing transactions so that everybody knows they came from us and not somebody who knows our address pretending to be us in order to spend our money. So far, so good, right? Not so fast... there's a problem.

Imagine I've sent you one of my UTXOs worth one bitcoin, as per our original example. It arrives in your wallet as a new input with no used outputs, available for you to spend. But what happens if I decide to be devious, unscrupulous, and outright dishonest, and I instruct my wallet software to send the *same* UTXO to another address? My second transaction would be sent out onto the network, and now everyone would see two different outputs from one input. How do we decide which is the real transaction? And how do we make sure everyone agrees on that decision?

Technically there is nothing preventing me from creating multiple transactions from the same UTXO. My wallet software, if properly constructed, shouldn't allow it, but I could create the transaction manually — it is just numbers after all. Even if I wasn't being deliberately duplicitous, there are scenarios in which wallets can become out of sync with the Bitcoin network and inadvertently try to send the same UTXO to a different address.

Re-using UTXOs is called *double-spending*, and obviously it cannot be allowed to happen, otherwise nobody will have any idea who really owns what. The whole system would come crumbling down. What then, do we do about the double spending problem? Enter...the blockchain!

The Blockchain

The blockchain is the innovation that makes cryptocurrencies like Bitcoin possible. It is the name given to the open ledger in which all transactions are recorded. Such a ledger cannot simply be a massive spreadsheet into which every transaction is entered when it is broadcast to the network, because that would leave us with the double-spending problem, and we'd have other problems too. How would we decide who has the power to write the transactions to the ledger? Bitcoin is supposed to be decentralised, but obviously it wouldn't be viable for everyone using the currency to update the ledger. If everyone could write entries, it would likely mean everyone could change them too. It would be chaos; impossible to trust. Yet if we nominated a set of trusted people to manage the blockchain, we would be centralising control of the currency.

The blockchain gets around these pitfalls. It cleverly allows for the transaction ledger to be decentralised, immutable, and trusted, all at the same time. Here's how it works. When a new transaction is sent out onto the Bitcoin network — passed around from node to node, spreading across the world — it eventually gets picked up by a special kind of Bitcoin node called a *miner*. There are lots of miners, and our transaction will be picked up by several. The miner will take our transaction box, and about 1500-2000 others like it, and they will wrap them all up into a big parcel of data called a *block*. Then they add a very long random number to the block (in technical terms, this random value is called a *nonce*, which if you're like me and are from the UK, may cause you to raise an eyebrow). Now the miner (or rather their computer) will take all the data that makes up the block and perform a special calculation on it called a *hash*. A hash calculation takes any piece of data and condenses it into a single very large number. If any part of the original data is changed — even just one letter — and the hash is re-calculated, the result will be completely different.

So our miner has lumped together anything up to about two thousand transactions (the exact number is not fixed and depends on the size of each transaction), added a nonce, and calculated a hash value that represents that whole block of data. If the hash value starts with a lot of zeros, their work is done. However, the chances of the hash starting with a lot of zeros is approximately one in 10^{19}. That's one in 100,000,000,000,000,000,000. If the hash result does not start with lots of zeros (which let's face it, is highly likely), the miner changes the nonce for a different random number and does the hash calculation again. And they keep trying, again and again, billions of times, until they stumble across a nonce that, when hashed with the rest of the block, gives an answer starting with lots of zeros. By the way, the reason I say 'lots' of zeros and not a specific number is because the number of zeros that are required changes over time. More on that later.

Although this hashing process is easy enough to do, it takes time. A lot of time. To put that 10^{19} number into some sort of context, looking for a nonce value that will end up giving the desired result is like trying to find one particular grain of sand among all the grains of sand on all the beaches on the planet (actually it's a bit harder even than that). It's such a difficult problem that if I tried to use my regular trading computer to accomplish the task, it would take roughly ten million years for it to do so.

Miners, as you might guess, do not use regular computers to perform these hash calculations. Instead they employ specially built machines that are designed for the purpose, and they use a *lot* of them. Even so, it's still a massively time and energy consuming task. There are enough miners working on the problem though, that roughly every ten minutes, someone somewhere will stumble across a nonce value that works for the block of transactions they have bundled together.

When that happens, that block is said to have been *mined* (or solved). The hash value the miner has found is added to the block, and the block is broadcast to the world. The transactions in that block are now said to have been *confirmed*, and the miner starts over with another block of transactions.

Anyone who can see the blockchain (which is everyone) can read the transactions in the newly mined block, and can read the nonce value that was included in it, and can calculate the hash value of that block themselves in the blink of an eye. They can compare it to the hash value the miner included in the block, confirm it matches, and conclude that the block has not been tampered with in any way. If the block had been altered, the result of the hash calculation would no longer match the one the miner attached to it.

If someone *did* want to fiddle with the transactions in the block — perhaps changing a destination address in a single large transaction to their own in order to enrich themselves — they would have to find a new nonce value that would produce another suitable hash result. As we've seen, that is an extraordinarily difficult task. It is also extraordinarily expensive because the cost of the electricity required mine a block runs into the thousands of dollars.

Even so, if someone was trying to redirect a transaction valued at *hundreds of thousands* of dollars to themselves, it might be worth their effort and expense to do that calculation.

Again, Satoshi Nakamoto thought of that, and this is where the *chain* in *blockchain* comes in. You see, there's one other vital piece of information that gets included in a block when it is mined, one I didn't mention before. Every block comprises not just a couple of thousand transactions and a nonce value, it also includes the hash value of the *previously mined block*. All the blocks that have ever been mined are linked together. The blockchain truly is a chain.

Think about that for a minute. If someone wanted to change a transaction in one block, they would have to re-mine not just that block, but also *every block that came after it*, because changing the hash of one block would break the hash of the next one, and so on, all the way down the chain.

The effort and expense of attempting to alter a block becomes greater with every block that is successfully mined after it. If it cost, say, ten thousand dollars in electricity to re-mine a block, it would cost twenty thousand to re-mine that block and the one that comes after it. And it would cost thirty thousand dollars to re-mine three blocks. Any fraudster attacking the blockchain would also have to re-mine each block in under ten minutes, otherwise they would never catch up with the new blocks being added to the end of the chain. After a very short time it becomes all but impossible to alter any given block because there are simply not sufficient computing resources in the world for it to be viable to re-mine enough blocks quickly enough.

The fact that blocks of transactions cannot be changed once they have been mined (we say they are immutable) solves our *double-spending* problem neatly. As soon as any one of our transactions that reuses the same output has been mined, i.e. confirmed within a block, any of the other transactions that attempt to spend the same Unspent Transaction Output can be immediately deemed invalid by the network. The wallet that originated the duplicate transactions will be informed they were rejected, and everyone can move on with their lives.

What's In It For The Miners?

Mining bitcoin doesn't just cost a fortune in electricity to power the super-powerful arrays of computers fast enough to have a chance of finding a working nonce value for a given block of transactions, those machines also cost a lot of money to buy in the first place. And because the machines get really hot, they also need to be run in air-conditioned environments, adding to the expense. A miner then, is spending considerable sums of money to try to find a random number that will confirm a block, and the chances are high that some other miner will find it before they do. The obvious question is: what's in it for the miner? Why go to the trouble and expense of mining the blockchain? Surely these people aren't donating their resources for the good of the Bitcoin economy?

The answer to that question explains how mining gets its name. When a miner successfully solves a block, they are given a reward. That reward is (at the time of writing), twelve and a half brand spanking new bitcoins. As long as the value of those bitcoins is greater than the average amount of money it costs a miner to 'win' them, they are quids in.

If you have been following along, you might have spotted a potential flaw in the bitcoin mining system. Bitcoin came into being in 2009. In the history of information technology and computing, that's a very long time ago. Computers have got much faster since then. The phone in your pocket is probably more powerful than the average desktop computer that was around in 2009. If mining bitcoin consumed vast computing resources nearly ten years ago, surely the machines available today can make short work of the job? Yet again, Satoshi Nakamoto foresaw the problem. The way they fixed it was two-fold. Firstly, they set up Bitcoin such that it becomes progressively harder to mine a block over time. Remember I said the miner must find a hash value that starts with a lot of zeros, and that the exact number of zeros wasn't fixed? It's because the required number of zeros increases periodically. Today a miner has to find a hash that starts with more zeros than was necessary in 2009. Every extra zero required makes mining a block exponentially harder. So even as computers get faster, mining remains relatively as difficult a task.

Of course, computers don't just get faster, they get cheaper too. So to disincentivise miners from throwing extra hardware at the mining problem (which would potentially make it possible to mine a disproportionate number of blocks and therefore gain overall control of the blockchain), the reward for successfully mining a block of transactions gets smaller over time. In 2009 the reward was 50 bitcoin. Today it is 12.5 bitcoin. At around the end of May 2020, the payout will be cut in half to 6.25 bitcoin. And once another 210,000 blocks have been mined, it will half again.

When twenty-one million bitcoins have been produced, there will be no more bitcoin reward. As we said at the start, bitcoin is designed to be a finite resource, like gold. There will only ever be twenty-one million in existence. We're not there yet — at the time of writing a shade under seventeen million bitcoin have been created. It will be a few years before the mining reward disappears completely.

Transaction Fees

Dwindling rewards, which will eventually disappear altogether, might make mining seem like a mug's game. Fortunately for miners, there is second incentive for solving blocks. When we send bitcoin, we include a small *fee* in the transaction. This fee forms another *output* in our transaction box, like this.

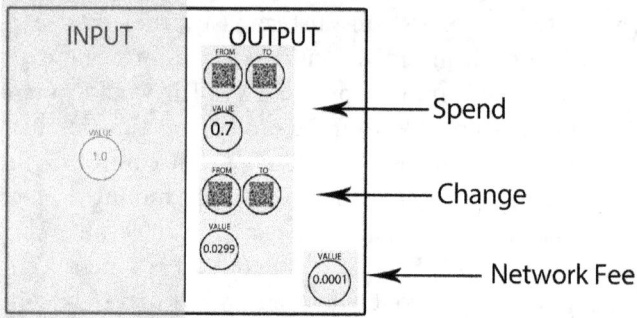

The miner who successfully solves a block is rewarded with all the fees from all the transactions in that block, as well as some new bitcoins.

How much we decide to pay as a fee depends on two things:

- How busy the Bitcoin network is.
- How fast we want our transaction to be confirmed in a block.

If the Bitcoin network is inactive, if there are very few transactions waiting to confirm, we can probably get away with paying a small fee. Miners will be obliged to include our transaction in their block because there aren't any others.

Most of the time though, there is a backlog of transactions waiting to be confirmed. It stands to reason that miners will choose those with the highest fees first when picking transactions to include in a new block so they earn more money. We can think of the fee as being a bit like a bid in an auction to get our transaction confirmed. The more transactions we outbid, the quicker ours will be picked up and mined.

Most modern wallets will analyse the state of the Bitcoin network in real time and suggest a fee that will get the transaction confirmed quickly. Some will suggest a range of fees, allowing us to choose a compromise between our our budget and the time we're willing to wait for confirmation.

Why Bitcoin?

For us as traders, Bitcoin's nature endows it with some attractive attributes, some that are less appealing, and some that are decidedly double-edged. Let's take a look at the positive side first.

24/7

Bitcoin never closes. That means potential trading opportunities can come along at any time of day or night, any day of the year. Unlike regular forex, which trades 24/5, Bitcoin takes no notice of weekends or bank holidays. The market can be as active at 3AM on a Sunday morning as it is at 9AM on Monday. For a trader who works full time but who wants to trade in their downtime, or for a trader whose local time zone is at odds with the traditional financial markets' time zones, this is a huge advantage. We can log into a bitcoin exchange any time of the day, any day of the week, and have the same chance of seeing a great trade setup.

Volatile

Bitcoin has seen enormous swings in value against the dollar, particularly in 2017 when it closed the year more than 1,300% up. For short-term trading, volatility means opportunity. There's no profit to be had from an instrument that flatlines day after day. Bitcoin's volatility works across all timescales, so provided your account balance and tolerance for risk can handle it, there are opportunities to be had for the scalper, day trader, and for anyone who wants to hold for days or weeks.

Unregulated

The stock markets are heavily regulated, particularly in the US. These regulations may govern the minimum size of a trading account, whether you can short a stock, and so on. Futures markets also have comprehensive oversight. Forex is more lax, but there are nonetheless rules and regulations about how much foreign currency an individual can hold.

Cryptocurrencies like Bitcoin have none of this oversight. Literally anyone can create a Bitcoin wallet. It is entirely possible to move money into and out of bitcoin without ever dealing with a corporation, bank, or government agency. If you do deal with a company (and for conventional trading opportunities, you will), that company sets their own rules about minimum account sizes. Note though that when a company like a bitcoin exchange has a relationship with a commercial bank for the purposes of moving customers' funds, they *are* likely to be regulated under common 'Know Your Customer' type rules designed to prevent money laundering (something that, not unsurprisingly, is common in the Bitcoin world). Therefore if you wish to open a trading account with a reputable exchange, you're still probably going to have to verify your identity.

That said, generally speaking, almost anyone can trade bitcoin regardless of their age or location[9]. There are no minimum account sizes, and no massive financial exchanges acting as gatekeepers to price data.

---

9 - The earlier disclaimer applies. Bitcoin is regulated in some countries and banned altogether in others. Please do your own due diligence about the legality of cryptocurrency in your country of residence.

Toolset

Whilst cryptocurrency may be a relatively recent invention, the toolset available to trade it has evolved quickly. Being unregulated, there is no central crypto exchange in the way there are stock and futures exchanges. That means there are no brokers in the traditional sense. Cryptocurrencies are traded like any other currency — on the forex model — with specialist currency exchanges providing decentralised marketplaces in which traders can participate.

There is a good selection of exchanges offering the high quality charting, order book, and even mobile tools a modern trader would expect. With no central exchanges holding the keys to price data, these tools are generally free to access. The exchanges make their money from the spread rather than account management fees.

We'll take a deeper look at exchanges later in the book.

Margin

Most exchanges offer margin trading, giving the trader leverage. Three times margin is usual, and more can be had by shopping around. Naturally, all good traders know that margin is a double-edged sword as it does not discriminate between profits and losses, multiplying both with equal ease.

Unconventional Trading Opportunities

The exchanges allow us to trade bitcoin the way we'd trade any other stock, future, commodity, or currency. But bitcoin is different, and its unique nature opens up other avenues for profit. These unconventional trading methods will be explored in their own chapter.

Why Not Bitcoin?

Okay, we've seen the good stuff. Your appetite has been whetted, you're raring to get going. Before you do, allow me to, if not burst, at least deflate your bubble a little. Bitcoin isn't all rainbows and unicorns, there are some snakes that go along with those ladders. Some of the ladders *are* snakes... Let's dive in before this mixed metaphor gets out of hand.

24/7

"But Harvey," I hear you cry. *"That was in the good stuff list."* Indeed it was. And it's here too, the first of the double-edged swords.

One of the great things about a market that doesn't operate around the clock is that it has an open and a close. These fixed points in time provide a certain amount of predictability, and some predictability is good. For example, as you'll know if you've read my book *How To Day Trade Stocks For Profit*, when the stock market opens in the morning, all the news that happened overnight gets traded in, potentially causing massive volatility and liquidity. It's not unusual for a news stock to trade as much volume in the first hour as it does in the rest of the day. Seasoned stock traders can pretty much guarantee a good selection of opportunities in the first hour of the day, and in the last hour too, as the market scrambles to consolidate its positions before the close.

Compare and contrast to a market that never closes. News and events are traded as they happen. There is no pent-up energy waiting to be released in one go. A good thing? Yes, if you can be in front of a screen for large chunks of the day to watch for the trades as they come along. But if your trading window is squeezed between coming home from work and going to bed, then some days there just may not be any trades to be had.

Whether the always-open nature of Bitcoin is a good or bad thing depends on the individual trader and their circumstances. It can mean more, or less, opportunity.

Unregulated

Here I go again, another one on both lists. Look, you've read the chapter on why *Bitcoin Is Different*. You know the risks. To reiterate, bitcoin is not legal tender, there is no central issuing authority overseeing the market, and there are no government backed guarantees. There are more ways to lose your shirt trading cryptocurrencies than there are trading just about anything else. An exchange could fold, taking your account balance with it. Mistakes can happen in transfers, losing bitcoins to the ether (or some unsuspecting benefactor's account). If you lose the password to your wallet, your money is gone. If someone steals your private key, your money is gone. If the exchange you trade on is hacked, your money is gone. In February 2014, the then largest bitcoin exchange in the world, Mt Gox, an exchange that handled an estimated 70% of all bitcoin trades at the time, closed its doors and quietly folded. 850,000 bitcoins disappeared. Back then, the losses were enormous. When you look at the price of bitcoin over 2017, they were even more enormous! The point is, lack of regulation giveth, and lack of regulation taketh away. All trading comes with risk. Bitcoin trading comes with additional risk. Understand it, and manage it accordingly.

Unpredictable News Cycle

Forex, stock, and futures prices are all affected by the news cycle. Official government figures like unemployment and inflation have a big impact. Earnings news on stocks is guaranteed to move the price. These news releases are all set out well in advance, allowing us to be in front of our trading station at the crucial moment, ready to pounce and trade the effect whatever it may be.

Bitcoin isn't like that. It is affected by news, but it's affected by the unpredictable kind. Exchange got hacked and customers lost millions? The price will almost certainly fall in the short term. But unless you happen to be the exchange's press officer, you're not going to have a clue about such an explosive press release until it's out there.

That's not to say that programmed news releases like unemployment figures can't affect the cryptocurrency market, they can. But their effect is so minimal as to not be worthy of consideration. Maybe that will change over time if Bitcoin becomes a bigger part of the economy.

Whether you see the lack of a predictable news cycle as good or bad depends on the kind of trader you are. Those who are risk averse may well choose to put this item on the list of positives.

Lack Of Liquidity

This is a generalisation, but bitcoin is far less liquid than most major currencies. The mechanics of the blockchain enforce hard limits on how many trades can be executed[10]. It may not always be easy or even possible to get out of bitcoin and into another currency at short notice.

---

10 - Although the number of transactions in a block isn't fixed, the size of a block is fixed at 1,000,000 bytes. The time taken to mine a block and the number of transactions that can be fitted into one give us an upper limit of about seven confirmed transactions per second.

The bigger exchanges mitigate the situation in the same way a CFD broker or forex exchange works: they make their own market, matching trades internally and hedging their positions in the wider market. Thus your bitcoin trade may never set foot inside the blockchain, happening instead entirely within the accounts of the exchange. But a lack of liquidity in the wider market will ultimately have an effect on the exchange's own ability to hedge, so it cannot be completely ignored.

High Fees

It used to be the case that we could fire off a bitcoin transaction worth thousands of dollars, pay just a few cents in network fees, and see the transaction confirm within twenty minutes. Sadly those days are long gone, at least for now. As Bitcoin has exploded in popularity, as its price has rocketed, so the network has become more congested, forcing up fees. The nature of the blockchain and the mining process and the increase in power required to make the whole system work has also contributed to the problem. It costs almost as much in electricity to mine new bitcoins as the bitcoins are worth. For a transaction to be worth a miner's time, the fee must be high. High fees kill profitability.

This issue isn't necessarily as bad as it sounds. Firstly, as mentioned above, many trades will never touch the blockchain so fees aren't an issue except when initially funding an account. So if we only trade conventionally, on an exchange, we may never have to worry about rising fees.

Secondly, there are moves afoot to alleviate the limiting nature of the blockchain. One such initiative is the Lightning Network. This proposed system will group together multiple small transactions into a larger one that is written to the blockchain, the cost being split between participants. It may never see the light of day, but if Lightning doesn't happen, something else like it probably will.

Third, Bitcoin is not the only cryptocurrency. If fees become a barrier, there's no shortage of alternatives out there that offer all the same advantages at a fraction of the cost.

Exchanges Are Islands

Like forex exchanges, cryptocurrency exchanges are islands of independence. They make their own prices, which means it's possible for an exchange to ignore the trend and stubbornly refuse to shift their price.

Every cloud has a silver lining, and in this case that lining is arbitrage. If one exchange is too out of sorts with the consensus, an arbitrage opportunity exists.

Also alleviating the island problem is the fact that most exchanges allow you to extract your funds in any currency you like, unlike forex exchanges which ask you to choose a base currency when you open your account. So if you just bought a load of monero with your bitcoin, and saw the price of monero rise against bitcoin everywhere except on your exchange, you wouldn't be stuck waiting for them to follow suit. You could simply transfer your new monero balance to an external wallet, or to another exchange, and trade it for bitcoin elsewhere.

Relatively Little Choice

There are literally hundreds of cryptocurrencies and new ones are popping up all the time. Compared to stocks though, choice is limited. Of the hundreds of coins that exit, many are worthless — either too illiquid to be tradable, too unstable, or simply too dubious in origin. Realistically, we're looking at dozens of coins, not hundreds. If you've come from the world of futures or forex, that won't phase you. But if you're used to a universe of tens of thousands of stocks to pick from, the lack of choice may seem limiting.

Ecological Concerns

As of early 2018, it takes about one bitcoin's worth of electricity to earn a bitcoin[11]. That's thousands of dollars-worth of electricity. If we break it down to a transaction level, the electricity required to mine a *single* bitcoin transaction would power an average house for twenty-four hours. In this age of ecological concerns and global warming, Bitcoin flies in the face of any effort to save energy. The amount of power being burnt by miners and their vast arrays of computers is roughly the same as is used by the entire country of Denmark, and it's only growing. Is all that power coming from renewable sources? Unlikely, especially when we consider that an increasing proportion of mining is being done in China, a country that whilst it is rapidly turning to greener methods of generation, is still primarily based on burning coal. Whether any of this bothers a given trader is obviously down to them, but it is certainly something to be aware of.

Amateur Hour

By way of its unregulated nature, Bitcoin attracts amateurs. Not just amateur traders, but service providers too. Earlier I mentioned Mt Gox, an exchange that at its height accounted for more than two-thirds of the world's bitcoin transactions. You might imagine that an exchange of such proportions was staffed by a huge team of skilled graduates overseen by managers drawn from the financial elite and backed with millions of dollars of venture capital. The reality couldn't be more different. Mt Gox was created by a sole programmer with time on his hands, a passing inter-

---

[11] - The actual cost depends on the cost of electricity in the country in which the mining is occurring. Obviously electricity prices vary greatly around the world.

est in Bitcoin, and zero experience of the world of finance. He soon sold it to someone equally poorly qualified to be running the show. Its demise was inevitable.

Even those who should know better can be caught out when setting up a new Bitcoin business. Bitpay, a sort of Bitcoin-Paypal, lost a small fortune when a hacker launched a 'phishing' attack on its chief financial officer[12]. Armed with the CFOs email password, the hacker transferred 5000 bitcoins out of Bitpay's wallet. It subsequently transpired that the insurance policy Bitpay had taken out against being hacked, and which it had trumpeted to its customers as a great feature, did not in fact cover them because their computers were never actually hacked; the attacker had used the CFOs password to make the transfer. Good intentions are no substitute for experience.

A point that was also made when startup bitcoin futures exchange Deribit found itself sitting on a quarter of a million dollar loss when a bug in their software caused it to go into a continuous loop. Deribit managed to put things right, and they ate the loss themselves. Other exchanges have not dealt with matters so ethically. More than one has chosen to 'socialise' losses from hacking — a silly euphemism for taking money out of client accounts to cover their own deficit.

Because anyone can set up an exchange, anyone will. That's not to say there aren't venture-backed businesses run by people who know what they're doing — there absolutely are. It is though, important to be aware of the risks in this new world.

Cryptocurrency attracts scammers and thieves. The amount of money pouring through the system paints a

---

12 - A phishing attack is when a hacker pretends to be someone else in order to obtain a victim's password. We've probably all seen phishing emails that try to get us to click on a link that looks like it's from PayPay or a bank, but is actually a dodgy URL waiting to steal our password.

huge target on its back for hackers, and I'm not just talking about bored adolescents sitting in their bedrooms trying to figure out how to steal a few bucks. North Korea, starved of funds due to international sanctions, is suspected of being behind some truly monumental hacks, including the 2018 theft of $425 million-worth of NEM coins from Japanese exchange Coincheck. It's the ideal crime for a desperate despot — the money is hard to trace and readily convertible into friendly US dollars, or anything else a cash-hungry dictator could want.

Child Abuse

Didn't expect that as a heading, did you? I certainly didn't expect to write it, but there we are. The sad fact of the matter is that the blockchain at the heart of Bitcoin has, according to researchers in Germany[13], had images of child abuse saved within it. This is possible because the Bitcoin protocol allows for additional non-financial data to be stored alongside transactions. Normally this space is for information like special payment instructions to be stored with the funds themselves, but literally any data can be written to the blockchain.

The nature of the pictures the researchers found makes possession of them illegal in many countries including the USA and the UK. Therefore it could conceivably be considered illegal to possess a copy of the blockchain. As we already know, we don't need a copy of the blockchain to use Bitcoin, but anyone carrying out mining does require at least part of it to be on their computer. And we also know that the blockchain is immutable — any images in there are there forever, they can't be deleted. We have to consider the possibility that in the future, the illegal and abhorrent photographs the researchers have discovered

---

13 - See: https://www.theguardian.com/technology/2018/mar/20/child-abuse-imagery-bitcoin-blockchain-illegal-content

may make bitcoin mining impossible without breaking the law. The consequences of such an eventuality would be far reaching, and could ultimately end with the demise of the currency.

Don't Despair

I may have painted a bleak picture in this last section, and there is no doubt cryptocurrency is a minefield. But the same is usually true of any exciting new opportunity. The key thing for any trader wishing to get into trading bitcoin to remember is to have their wits about them, assume nothing, trust nobody, and tread carefully. Kind of a rule for life in general.

Wallets

We've seen how Bitcoin behaves like cash and how like cash, it needs a wallet to be kept in. Unlike cash, the wallet (sometimes also called a client) is not optional. Not only is it compulsory, it's part of the system; it's how Bitcoin works.

We already know that a Bitcoin wallet, at its core, comprises three things: a public key, a public address (derived from the key) to which transactions can be sent, and a related private key used to sign outbound transactions. We could get away with just these three components, but there's a problem. If we always use the same address for sending and receiving bitcoin, anyone could monitor all of our transactions by looking at the blockchain. Our financial history becomes an open book.

To mitigate this issue, we use multiple addresses. Ideally we want to use a new address every time we transact. This keeps every transaction sandboxed, making it roughly impossible for any one person we transact with to trace back our history and see all our other transactions.

If we only ever trade conventionally through an exchange, we can use the wallet provided by that exchange. *This is not recommended!* Remember, in the world of cryptocurrency, whoever holds the keys holds the cash. A wallet at an exchange is under the control of the exchange — its private key is stored on their computers. There is nothing stopping the people behind the exchange getting greedy and running off with all the coin under their control. It has happened before. Okay, strictly speaking the law is there to prevent that sort of thing, but Bitcoin's nature makes such thefts an easy crime to get away with.

For long-term storage of funds then, we are better off with our own wallet — one under our control and only ours.

There are two main types of wallet, hot and cold. A hot wallet is one that is connected to the internet. Coins can be transacted directly from the wallet. Cold wallets or cold storage on the other hand, are kept offline. There are advantages and disadvantages to hot and cold wallets, and there are different kinds of each too, so let's have a look in more detail.

Hot Wallets

Any wallet that is connected to the internet is a hot wallet. There are two categories of hot wallet.

Software Wallet

This can be an app on a mobile device, or an application (program) on a computer. A software wallet manages your bitcoin on your device. It will generate addresses that funds can be sent to, and can send funds to addresses you enter into it, creating transactions and sending them out into the world to be confirmed by miners and locked into the blockchain.

When we first use a software wallet, it will create a unique address and an associated public/private key pair. Usually we never need to those keys, they will be stored securely inside the app. To prevent anyone else from accessing your funds, we secure the app with a PIN number or a password, or in some cases with biometric methods such as a fingerprint or facial scan, if the device supports it.

Earlier I explained why we want to avoid reusing Bitcoin addresses. Our software wallet should be able to generate new addresses on demand. Every time a new address is created, there will be a new key pair that goes along with it. But this presents us with a new problem. Because our wallet exists only as data on a phone or computer, it is vulnerable to all the same potential data-eating problems as our other data, like our photos or emails. If we drop our phone down the toilet, or the battery explodes, or someone steals it, we lose access to the data, which means we lose access to the funds in our wallet. Fortunately we already know how to mitigate the risks of digital destruction — we have backups. We should regularly backup whatever device our software wallet resides on. That might mean connecting a phone to a computer and copying its contents to the hard drive, or we might have online backups that are done automatically to the 'cloud' (iPhones do this, for example).

A backup will save us if there's a problem with our device, but what about if the wallet itself suffers from an issue? Software is fallible. It can break. Apps can be pulled from app stores without notice. If we're entrusting money to the care of an app, we need to be certain we can access those funds no matter what, including if the app ceases to be. Thus it is highly advisable to store enough information to be able to recreate a given wallet, somewhere safe. The information required to recreate a wallet is its address and private key (the wallet software can work out the public key by itself, given these other details). The storage method might be as simple as writing both down on a piece of paper and putting it somewhere secure (see the section on paper wallets later in this chapter). But ideally every time we transact in bitcoin we create a new address and a new private key to go with it. That means if we want our backup to be truly comprehensive, we will need to update it with these new pieces of information every single time we send or receive money. Cumbersome to say the least, but back in the early days of Bitcoin it was the only option for keeping a wallet safe.

Fortunately Bitcoin does not sit still, it is an evolving beast. Evolution in the world of Bitcoin (and here I'm talking specifically about Bitcoin) happens through a recognised protocol for suggesting improvements to the system. These are called Bitcoin Improvement Proposals, or *BIP*s. A BIP tends to be very technical and detailed, certainly not light reading, and its ins and outs don't concern us. What's important is that proposal number 32 (BIP32) specifically deals with the problem of multiple addresses and how to keep track of them easily. The proposal has been adopted by the majority of mainstream software wallets. BIP32 introduces what are called *Hierarchical Deterministic* wallets (commonly abbreviated to HD wallets). That's a fancy term that means *"We can tell what's coming next by looking at what came before."*

In practice this means instead of our wallet dishing up an entirely random new address every time we want to transact, it creates new addresses in a predictable manner. As long as we know the starting point for a given wallet, it can recreate all the addresses it has ever generated, and will ever generate. And *that* means if we want to keep a backup of our HD wallet, all we haven'to store is the starting point; we don't need every address it has ever used.

To put this into context, imagine you have a ton of passwords for all the websites you visit, like your email, bank, online shopping, etc. If you used random password generation (which you should, by the way), then when you create a new account on a new website, you have no idea ahead of time what that password is going to be — it will only become known when you create it. To backup your passwords you would have to write down a list of every site you visit and the password that goes with it. If you wanted to make your life easier, you could use a deterministic system of creating passwords. For example, you might choose to use your middle name, followed by the day of the month you were born, followed by the first three letters of the website you are visiting. So if you created an account on eBay, your password might be 'john15eba'. And when you create a new account on Google, your password would be 'john15goo'. Instead of having to remember — and backup — loads of unrelated passwords, you would only have to remember the rule — middle name, day of month, first three letters of the website.

HD wallets are a lot more complicated than that behind the scenes, but the concept is the same. When an HD wallet is created it generates a random *seed* value (the starting point). From this seed, new addresses and private keys grow — being created in a deterministic way. All we have to backup is the seed. If we lose our wallet, it doesn't matter if it originated one transaction or one thousand, we could create a new wallet, re-enter our backed-up seed value, and it would regenerate all the addresses and pull in their associated transactions from the public blockchain. Once it was done, it would be an exact replica of what we had before.

HD wallets are generally a good thing, but you've probably spotted the flaw. Anyone who has the seed value to a wallet can recreate it, completely and fully, and will have total control over the funds within it. So our seed value should be treated with the same reverence and security as we would give the cash it is protecting.

Seed values for HD wallets are extremely long and random. A typical seed might look like this:

```
274ddc525802f7c828d8ef7ddbcc5304e87ac3535
 913611fbbfa986d0c9e5476c91689 9c8a54fd55d3
 8606aa6a8595ad213d4c9c9f9aca3 b217069a41028
```

Not exactly memorable, right? All the money in our wallet may depend on us not losing that bit of text. Fortunately we have another BIP to help us with this little problem. BIP39 proposes a system in which seed values are converted into a mnemonic code — that is to say, regular English words. The above seed converts to this:

```
ozone drill grab fiber curtain grace pudding
     thank cruise elder eight picnic
```

Much easier to deal with. You could probably even memorise it if you tried. It's simple to store twelve words, so there's no excuse not to.

With the seed value tucked away somewhere for safe keeping, we can recreate our software wallet at will. In theory, we could even move it from one app to another. However, this being the internet, everyone has their own ideas and software vendors are no exception. Although functionally HD wallets might all work the same way, under the hood there can be differences. We cannot assume that a 12-word mnemonic code will work the same from one app to the next.

Remember (yes, I'm going to keep banging on about this), treat your seed value as if it was cash. You probably wouldn't store thousands of dollars in bills in your kitchen cupboard; apart from the risk of someone wandering off with it, it could get damaged by fire or flood, or the cat could chew it up. Same goes for a wallet backup. Put it somewhere safe, like a safe. For even more security, split it up and keep it in multiple locations. It comprises twelve words[14], so perhaps keep six words in a safe, and another six in your holiday home, or in the car, or at a friend's house, or taped to the back of the garage door... You get the idea.

---

14 - Some wallets use a more secure implementation that translate to a seed mnemonic code of more than twelve words, and may be as many as twenty-four.

Software wallets are among the most flexible wallets available. Here are their main advantages:

- They are entirely under the owner's control. We are not entrusting our private keys to a third party, so provided we secure our wallet correctly, we don't need to worry about anyone wandering off with our cash.

- They offer high levels of anonymity. HD wallets generate new addresses every time we send or receive bitcoin, making it approximately impossible for anyone to track our activity beyond a single transaction. And because everything happens on our device, there's no corporation looking over our shoulder, or reporting our earning and spending habits to a marketing company, or a tax office[15].

- They manage our transactions as well as storing our funds. When we want to send someone some bitcoin, we type in their address, or more likely scan a QR code version of it, tell it how much we are sending, choose a network fee, and we're done. We can follow the transaction's progress right inside the app.

- They're convenient. A wallet app on a phone means bitcoin is always to hand.

The downsides of software wallets are few, but worthy of consideration too.

- A software wallet is, to all intents and purposes, a black box. We have to trust whoever makes it. The developer of a software wallet app could choose to write it in such a way that it secretly sends them a copy of our private keys. Some apps are open source, which is to say that the computer code that makes

---
15 - You should of course, report your earnings to your tax authority yourself.

them work is published and available for anyone to inspect, meaning those with the right know-how can verify there is nothing nefarious baked-in. We must also trust the app developer is competent and that their app won't break down or malfunction in some way and splatter our balance around the internet. For these reasons, it is advisable to choose a wallet from a reputable developer, one that has been independently audited if at all possible, and that is in wide use, suggesting any horrific bugs have already been found and dealt with.

• Software wallets are under our control — a benefit that can come back and bite us. If we mess up and lose our seed value mnemonic, we could lose our cash. It's our responsibility alone to secure our wallet.

• A software wallet is (usually) restricted to a single device. It is technically possible to have a copy on a second device, but it's not recommended because the two copies may not be perfectly synchronised at all times, and transactions would be rejected if two copies of the wallet try to *double spend* the same UTXOs.

There are software wallets for all main computing and smartphone platforms. Phone-based wallets are popular, but there are computer-based apps for Windows, Mac, and Linux machines too. Some examples of software wallets include:

• BRD [https://breadapp.com] (iOS and Android). Formerly known as *Bread*, and *Bread Wallet* before that, this is a popular choice for iPhones and iPads. Bread is very easy to use. It only offers two levels of network fee though, so seasoned traders who want more control may have to look elsewhere.

The code is not open source, but it has passed Apple's stringent app review process, and is widely used with no major reported bugs. Bread supports Bitcoin, Bitcoin Cash, and Ethereum.

• Electrum [https://electrum.org] (Windows, MacOS, Linux, Android, source code). A very popular open source wallet, though not the friendliest or easiest to use. Those with the know-how can download the source code, inspect it, and compile it themselves, ensuring nobody else could possibly have tampered with it. Electrum can keep its keys off-line for use as cold storage (see the section later in this chapter for more on cold storage). This wallet is slightly unusual in that rather than scan the blockchain directly to bring itself up to date, it uses servers to do some of the heavy lifting.

• Mycelium [https://wallet.mycelium.com] (iOS, Android). Not a fungus that enables instant interstellar travel[16], but a mobile Bitcoin wallet that claims to be the most popular of its kind. Like Electrum, Mycelium has its own servers that enable it to run faster as it doesn't need to process the entire blockchain on the device. Of course, this means trusting that those servers are not doing anything iffy with the transaction data passing through them.

Please note that none of these apps are recommendations, only examples. You should research any wallet you are interested in before downloading it to your computer or device.

---

16 - See Star Trek: Discovery

Online Wallet

An online wallet is a software wallet stored on a third party service rather than our own device. It often (though not always) offers an app component allowing access from a phone, and providing a means to transact. Because the wallet itself is stored somewhere on the internet, any app or web browser we use to manipulate it is only a window onto the wallet. Think of it as being like an email account that we can get at using our phone's email app as well as a website — the emails are all living on a server on the internet, the app and browser are merely a means of accessing them. We can have multiple windows into an online wallet in the same way. So we could have an app on our phone, another on a tablet, and a web browser accessing the wallet from a computer, all without any risk of double spending because they are all looking at the same data.

Online wallets have a number of advantages over software wallets.

- Our wallet can be accessed from anywhere with no risk of it trying to double spend, which would result in transactions being rejected.

- If our device crashes or breaks, it won't affect our wallet.

- Apps offered by the wallet provider are usually full-featured, making it just as easy to transact as a dedicated software wallet. They also tend to come with customer support, so there's somebody there if we need help.

- Those upsides are tempered by some not inconsiderable risks.

- We don't have ultimate control over the keys. An online wallet might let us see our private key or seed mnemonic (and we should certainly try to choose one that does), but the people running it have access to that data too. And we know what that means by now. They control the key, so they control the funds.

• Because the wallet is stored on someone else's server — connected to the internet — it is at risk of being hacked. Much as that might sound like the sort of thing that happens in movies but not real life, the sad truth is cryptocurrency wallets get hacked with alarming frequency.

• Hackers aren't the only bad actors who can ruin our day; errant employees of the wallet provider could access our funds. It has happened before, and will undoubtedly happen again.

If you choose to use an online wallet, you are choosing a compromise of ease of use over security. The risks all come down to the fact someone else is in control. It almost goes without saying, but I'll say it anyway — do your due diligence before putting money into an online wallet. Stick to bigger, well known tried and tested providers. Don't be the guinea pig who tries out the new service only to discover it's a scam. If you are entrusting your hard-earned money to someone, you need to be as sure as you can be that you can trust them. Look for evidence of independent audits and quality assurance. And if they have insurance against loss, so much the better.

Here are two examples of well known software wallets. Again, these are not recommendations, merely a starting point for your own due diligence and research.

• Blockchain.info is probably the best known software wallet, and they claim to be the most popular in the world with over twenty-two million accounts. Blockchain offers a number of digital currency services in addition to their wallet product.

The company has backing from big-name investors including Virgin. They have iPhone and Android apps as well as a good web interface. The wallet supports both Bitcoin and Ethereum. Through a network of exchange partners it is possible to buy and sell bitcoin from within the app.

• Coinbase [https://www.coinbase.com] also claims to be the most popular online wallet. It too has millions of accounts, apps for both major mobile platforms (iOS and Android), and has raised even more venture capital than Blockchain.info, also from some very big names. Coinbase claims that wallet funds are protected by an insurance policy which covers hacking of their servers or theft by an employee, though it does not insure against unauthorised access of individual accounts. So if Bob from their marketing department does a runner with your bitcoin, you will probably be okay. But if you leave your password lying around and your aunt uses it to steal your balance, that's down to you. Coinbase supports Bitcoin, Bitcoin Cash, Ethereum, and Litecoin. As an exchange, Coinbase also enables buying and selling of cryptocurrency.

Cold Wallets / Cold Storage

Cold storage is any kind of wallet that is not *online*, i.e. not connected to the internet. The two most common forms of cold storage are paper wallets and hardware wallets. By keeping a wallet offline, we are keeping it safe from hackers and other bad actors who could otherwise access it, such as errant exchange employees or dodgy developers of wallet apps.

Paper Wallet

A paper wallet is exactly what it sounds like — a wallet stored on paper. And you thought Bitcoin was high-tech! If we think about what a wallet actually is — a public address and a private key that signs transactions from it — it becomes obvious that this pair of assets can be stored in any form, not just digitally. Heck, we could carve them into a stone tablet if we really wanted to. A paper wallet then, is a medium onto which we have physically written or encoded in some way, a Bitcoin address and the private key that signs it.

You could say a paper wallet is the ultimate means of exercising complete control over our bitcoin. It makes the digital currency as close to real cash as it can be — it's literally paper money. But even paper wallets are not without risks, as we'll see.

A paper wallet is, obviously, a static object not a functional one. We can't look at it and see how much bitcoin is stored in the address. It can, however, receive funds, and can be used to send funds.

To receive bitcoin, we share the public address with anyone who needs to send money to the wallet. But how do we know if the funds arrived? The piece of paper isn't going to change magically when money hits the wallet. We can't tell from looking at the paper, but we can look at the blockchain, which is after all a public ledger. One way to do that would be to use a blockchain exploration tool like blockchain.info (another service they offer). On the front page of that website is a box into which we can enter our public address, and the tool will return the balance of bitcoin sent to that address, the number of transactions, and for each transaction it will tell us the sending address and the amount sent. If we enable the advanced view, we can even see the fee paid to the network, as well as the inputs used by the sender.

Another way to check the balance of our paper wallet would be to import the public address into a wallet app. If the app lets us import the address without importing the private key (something both Electrum and Mycelium support), it becomes a read-only wallet — a window into the activity of the address without any means of signing transactions. Thus our paper wallet remains cold.

Let's say we wanted to take some of our trading profits and keep them in cold storage. We decide a paper wallet is the way to go. Our first action is to create a new Bitcoin address and private key to sign it. Unless we happen to be a mathematical genius with a lot of time on our hands, we're going to need some help coming up with an address. Fortunately help is at hand. There are websites and apps that will happily create new addresses for us at the click of a button. Bitaddress.org is one of the most well known, and another is coinb.in.

Before we go and create our paper wallet, there is an important safety consideration. The whole point of a paper wallet is that we want an address nobody else can possibly know about, and that does not require us to trust a third-party like an app developer or exchange. Yet the very first step in creating one requires us to trust the bitaddress.org or coinb.in websites. How do we know that every address and private key they generate is not being saved to a database somewhere, for the site developer to pillage later at their leisure? The short answer is we don't. The long answer is we sort of do, but it's complicated. These websites are open source — the code that makes them work is available for those who understand it to inspect. It's digitally signed, too, so we can be sure the code open for inspection is the code that's actually running on the website. If we trust that the community has audited the code, then we have nothing to worry about, right? Well, yes and no. We're still delegating trust, it's just we've transferred our trust to an unknown community of developers. And there's more. Websites can be hacked. Criminals can hijack internet connections and steal data passing between our computer and the website, or they can even redirect us to a copy of the website they are running, but which has been modified to steal keys. In short, unless we happen to be extremely technically savvy, we cannot fully trust a website.

Luckily, those clever people who made these sites foresaw the problem and designed them in such a way that we can use them without being connected to the internet. All we have to do is load the site, disconnect our WiFi, and then generate our paper wallet.

Here's how that works in practice. Let's say we choose to use coinb.in, because it's quick and simple. We go to the site, click on 'New' in the top menu, and choose 'Address'. Once the page has loaded, we switch off our WiFi, or pull out the network cable from our computer, or turn off the data connection on our phone. If we're using a mobile device, putting it into Airplane Mode will work. Only then do we hit the 'Generate' button. Hey presto, coinb.in will give us an address and private key. Hit 'Generate' again and it will give us another. Because we're not connected to the internet, we don't have to worry about anyone intercepting the data and storing it for their own use.

We write down the address and private key — taking extra care not to make any mistakes — and if we want, we can get a QR code too by clicking on the little code icon next to the address. The QR code makes it easier to receive bitcoin to the address later. Then we close down the browser window before reconnecting to the internet.

Can we now be sure that nobody else has this address and key? Unfortunately there is still a caveat or two. It's possible the computer we are using has been infected with malware that is spying on us. Good up-to-date antivirus software can help here. If we use an Apple iOS device that has not been 'jailbroken', we can be fairly sure we are malware free. The same cannot be said for Android devices unfortunately, as they are hotbeds of spyware and other dubious apps that can do all sorts of underhand things. Even assuming we are malware free, we are still trusting that coinb.in's website has generated a truly unique address and private key, and has not been programmed to dish out pre-determined keys that are already stored away. Ultimately, unless we are willing to download the code running the site (which coinb.in allows and encourages) and have the technical nous to audit it ourselves and run it locally, we are always going to have to trust someone, somewhere along the line. The good news is that hundreds of thousands of paper wallets are generated by these two websites, and I've yet to hear of a single reason to suspect they are anything but entirely honest. As always, do your own research.

Okay, so we've created our address and key, and have written them down without anyone looking over our shoulder. We have a paper wallet, but it's empty. Now we can head to our bitcoin exchange account (see the next chapter for more on exchanges), type in our new address or scan our QR code, and send our trading profits to our paper wallet for safe keeping. Then we go to blockchain.info and enter our public address there to see when the money arrives. Our private key is not stored in an app, or on anyone's web server. We never need worry about a North Korean state-sponsored hacker getting it and making off with our balance.

That's not to say paper wallets are without risk. If we go for a literal *paper* wallet, it would be prudent to consider that paper is not a robust or durable medium. Unless we keep it in a climate and humidity-controlled environment like the Vatican library, we cannot expect it to last indefinitely. It can burn, tear, shred, and be chewed by mice. Ink can run, pencil can be erased, and both can be obscured by someone scrawling on top of whatever is written on it. This is probably not a problem if our wallet only contains a few dollars-worth of bitcoin, but it's more of a worry if we're saving thousands of dollars offline. We should also remember that if anyone sees the private key to a wallet, they can access it and spend it. So we wouldn't want to store our paper wallet anywhere someone might steal a glance at it, or be able to photograph it. We should treat our paper wallet as if it were cash, because that is almost exactly what it is. If we've got ten dollars-worth of bitcoin in it, we should treat it like a ten dollar bill. If we've got ten thousand dollars-worth in it, well, we should treat it like a ten thousand dollar bill!

So far so good, but what happens when we want to spend some of the money in our paper wallet? Or transfer it into an exchange so we can trade with it? It might be as valuable as cash, but if we decide to go and buy a new car, it's unlikely the dealer will accept it in payment.

We have three options for spending a paper wallet. First, we *could* actually hand it to someone as payment. With the address and key we have written down, the recipient could transfer the funds wherever they wanted (this is called *sweeping* the wallet or sweeping the balance). The recipient would have to agree to take bitcoin in payment, and it would be best if the wallet balance corresponded exactly with the payment amount so there was no messing around with change in the traditional sense. The recipient would also likely want to check the wallet really contained the funds we said it did, perhaps by using a blockchain explorer like blockchain.info. And they'd have to sweep the funds immediately, in case we had sneakily kept a photocopy somewhere and were planning on sweeping it ourselves before they got the chance. All in all, handing over a paper wallet as remittance for goods or services is unlikely to happen.

A better way to spend the contents of the wallet would be to sweep it ourselves. Importing the address and private key into a wallet app or online wallet would convert our cold paper wallet into a regular hot wallet. We'd then be free to spend it however we wanted. But what if we didn't want to transfer the entire balance into hot storage? What if we only wanted to move half? In this case we have two options. First, we could transfer everything to a hot wallet, create a new paper wallet, and transfer half the balance back to that. It's a bit cumbersome, and we'd be paying network fees to send money that was originally on paper, back to paper, but it is generally easier than the alternative.

That alternative, which is also the third way to spend bitcoin from cold storage, is to create a bitcoin transaction offline manually (keeping our wallet cold), and only once it is signed with our private key, connect to the internet to transmit it to the Bitcoin network. Here's how that works. I warn you now that this sounds harder than it is. If you try it, you'll see it's actually a simple step-by-step process. First, we head back to coinb.in (or another site offering the same service). We click 'New' on the menu and this time choose 'Transaction'. In the first box we enter the public address of our paper wallet (or scan the QR code if we made one), and click the 'Load' button. This will load in any UTXOs from our paper address — in our example case here this will be the single transaction in which we loaded up our paper wallet. Further down in the 'Output' section, we fill in the destination address and the amount we wish to send. If you read the chapter on how Bitcoin works you will remember that that every transaction input corresponds to zero or more outputs which are in turn connected to the next input, and that we cannot spend a fraction of a transaction that arrived in our paper wallet, we must spend all of it. This is at odds with our objective (we want to keep half the money) so we have to send the remainder of the balance back to ourselves as change. We do that by creating a second output (by clicking the '+' button) and adding in our own paper wallet address and the amount we want to retain, minus whatever the transaction fee is we want to attach to this transaction. Coinb.in will add up the two outputs, deduct them from the input used in the transaction, and assign the difference as the fee. If we forget to send the remainder of the balance back to our paper wallet, it will all be sent as a transaction fee and lost to us, so this step is very important. Next we hit 'Submit', and coinb.in will return some text that is our encoded transaction. It's almost ready to send out to the network. Almost, but not quite ready. For the transaction to be accepted, we must sign it with our private key to prove it really was us who made it. So we copy the transaction text that was returned in the green box, then click 'Sign' on the top menu, and paste it into the big text box provided. Now we go off-line, like we did when we created our paper wallet, to ensure no jiggery-pokery. We type the private key written on our paper wallet into the box at the top, check we made no errors, then click 'Submit'. The webpage will return more text, which is our signed transaction. Finally we copy that text to the clipboard, go back online, go to the 'Broadcast' menu item, paste in the transaction, hit 'Submit', and we're done.

I told you it was a bit long-winded! We've done exactly the same job a software wallet app does, just one step at a time, and mostly manually. As we were not connected to the internet at the one and only time we wielded our private key (when we signed the transaction), that key's integrity remains assured.

Brain Wallet

A paper wallet doesn't have to be kept on paper. For the ultimate in security, it can be memorised. Needless to say, that's quite a feat given the lengthy and meaningless sequences of digits that make up Bitcoin addresses and private keys, but it's doable, if you are willing to trust your funds to your memory.

At a minimum, a brain wallet involves remembering the private key — the address part can be written down. If the wallet is BIP39 compliant, turning it into a brain wallet is much easier as all we need to remember is the sequence of twelve (or more) words that represent the seed value. The downside of this method is that to spend or even receive money to such a wallet, those words will have to be entered into an app of some sort to recreate the wallet.

Hardware Wallet

If the idea of fiddling about with paper and manually creating wallets and transactions in order to manage your cold storage leaves you, well, a bit cold, there is an alternative method for keeping our earnings out of the hands of the hackers. It's called a hardware wallet, and like a paper wallet, it does exactly what it says on the tin.

A hardware wallet is a physical device that performs the same functions as a software wallet, but that is not connected to the internet — except when we want to transact. A hardware wallet is essentially a single-purpose computing device with some software smarts. That means it can work as an HD wallet, generating new addresses for every transaction and guarding our anonymity.

There are a few options for hardware wallets.

- A dedicated *air-gapped* computer. If we run a software wallet on a machine that has no internet connection, and that serves no other function than to act as a bitcoin store, it's a hardware wallet. When we want to send bitcoin, we hook up to the network, carry out our business, then disconnect. Air-gapping a dedicated machine is safer than keeping a hot wallet on general purpose hardware, but every time we connect it to the internet we run the risk of infection from malware, or other forms of hacking.

- A USB key. There are a few of ways of using a USB key as a hardware wallet. The simplest is to store a Bitcoin address and private key on it in the form of text files. In other words, to use it as an electronic version of a paper wallet. Or we could keep a software wallet on the key, using the key as a regular hard drive and plugging it into a computer and loading it up when we want to transact. Even better, we could make the USB key a bootable installation of a secure operating system. In this case, we would plug in the key, boot a computer from it, transact, then shut down. In this way, even if the host computer was infected with malware it wouldn't matter because we wouldn't be using the operating system installed on it. The risk of malware infection would be reduced to the few minutes the key was plugged in and booted. There are Linux installations which suit this purpose. The super-technical, who want to control everything, could conceivably even bake their own Linux install, compiling their own binaries after auditing the code to be certain there's nothing untoward going on, but that's way out of the reach of the average human being. Whichever form of USB wallet we used, we would of course want to protect the device by encrypting it and setting a password to access it.

• A dedicated hardware wallet device. If we're serious about keeping large amounts of bitcoin safe in cold storage, a dedicated hardware wallet is one of the best solutions. It's also the most expensive. Security comes at a price.

As dedicated hardware wallets are the safest option, we'll look at those in more detail.

A proper hardware wallet is a small physical device on which is kept the private key to our wallet's seed address (the address from which all others are generated). It works in conjunction with a software component on a computer. In order to send bitcoin, we must connect the device to our computer (usually via USB), then physically authorise the transaction by pressing buttons on the device. Everything on the device is encrypted, secured by a password or passphrase that we choose when we set it up. Because the wallet is a single-purpose hardware device that cannot be written to, it cannot be hacked. No malware can install itself on there, there's nowhere for it to go[17].

Some hardware wallets, like the Trezor, can store more than one wallet, and even hide wallets. We could, for example, keep a decoy wallet with a low balance, and a hidden wallet in which we have stashed our riches. If we were wishing to keep those riches hidden from an authority that had the power to force us to unlock the hardware wallet, this would be a good way to do so.

Hardware wallets, cool as they may be, are not a panacea for security. Firstly, devices like Trezor only work

---

17 - In theory. In March 2018, a 15-year-old researcher demonstrated how a popular hardware wallet called Ledger could be hacked, thereby also demonstrating how important it is to keep up with developments in the Bitcoin world for anyone invested in it.

with computers, not mobile devices, so are becoming increasingly limited as more people switch to mobile-only. As traders we probably all use regular computers so this might not be a concern for us, but for how long? We want our cold storage to be a lasting store of wealth. Secondly, we are still required to place trust in a third party — the manufacturer of the device. Again, we want it to be independently audited to be certain a rogue engineer hasn't planted a back door inside, or that the device isn't secretly transmitting our private keys to the company who manufactured it every time we plug it in. And finally we still have the issue of physical storage. Here's a thought experiment: what would happen if your local crime lord got wind of the fact you have a little device worth hundreds of thousands of dollars, and all they had to do to take the money was force you to hand over your password? Maybe that's far fetched. Maybe not. People get kidnapped and held to ransom, it happens. In most ransom cases the risk to reward ratio for the perpetrator is not great; they must collect cash without being caught, hope the money isn't marked, and launder it without it being traced. Contrast this with a ransom of a Bitcoin wallet where all they require is your password or secret mnemonic seed in order to vanish your funds without a trace, and suddenly that risk to reward ratio looks more appealing.

I'm overstating the risks to make a point. Ultimately it's up to the individual to choose the solution that meets their needs with the best compromise for them. Realistically, the risks are low, but we should always be aware of them.

Whatever we choose for a hardware wallet, we will want to keep a copy of its seed mnemonic backed up somewhere, separate from the device itself (and somewhere very secure — a bank deposit box perhaps). If the device is lost or falls into the wrong hands, we can replace it and recreate its contents from the seed, then sweep it into a new wallet, ensuring that if the original is attacked and decrypted, it will be empty.

Backup, Backup, Backup

This cannot be overstated, so I'll say it again: if we lose access to our wallet, whether hot or cold, we lose access to the funds inside — forever. Cryptocurrency wallets are not like online banking apps, giving a window into money stored securely in a nation-state-backed bank account. They *are* the money. No wallet, no money. The security of our bitcoin is our responsibility alone.

It is estimated that around 30% of all bitcoins mined to date have already been lost due to negligence, carelessness, or in some cases wilful destruction. Somewhere in a landfill site in the UK there's a hard drive containing the key to a wallet worth about $80 million (as of December 2017). The owner mined 7,500 bitcoins years ago when mining was cheap and easy and bitcoin almost worthless. When his computer stopped working, he broke it up and sold it for parts, but kept the hard drive in a drawer. Then in 2013, the drive got accidentally thrown away in a clear out. That money is probably lost forever now. It can never be re-mined[18], except by physically mining the landfill site in which it is assumed the drive ended up and hoping the data can be recovered. There is no shortage of cautionary tales like this — take care not to join them.

---

18 - Unless perhaps, one day we have quantum computers that can reverse engineer the whole system in the blink of an eye. But if that happens, cryptocurrencies will become worthless overnight anyway.

Exchanges

A cryptocurrency exchange is, perhaps obviously, a place where we can exchange cryptocurrency for fiat currencies or other cryptocurrencies, and vice versa. It functions much like any other foreign exchange service, swapping one currency for another and making a profit from the spread between the buy and sell prices, or by taking a commission, or both.

There are hundreds of exchanges out there, some big, some small, some operated by huge corporations, some run by kids in their bedrooms. Any exchange will have some common features.

- An online wallet. It is into this wallet that our bitcoin (or whatever coin we are working with) will be deposited by the exchange in return for the currency we are paying with. For the reasons we have already covered, it is wise to treat this wallet as a temporary holding area, not a place to store currency long term. The wallet is also a place where we can send bitcoin to the exchange in payment for another currency.

- A means for receiving fiat currency. If we are buying bitcoin, we'll need to pay for it somehow. Assuming we are paying with regular fiat currency, the exchange must offer a way to take our remittance. Common payment methods are credit and debit cards, and wire transfers. No reputable exchange currently accepts PayPal due to fraud concerns. That's not to say there are not ways and means of obtaining bitcoin with Paypal, there are, just not directly from an exchange.

- A way of extracting fiat currency. Exchanges work both ways. If we are selling bitcoin for dollars, pounds, euros or yen, we'll need a way to get that money out. Wire transfer is the most common method, but not the only one. Some exchanges offer prepaid debit cards that can be loaded up with the proceeds of our sale.

I mentioned it earlier in this book and it is worth repeating here, that whilst Bitcoin itself is largely unregulated in most markets, if an exchange has relationships with banks in order to accept and make wire transfers, it will in most cases find itself subject to anti-money laundering rules. That means rules like 'know your customer', in which the exchange is obliged to verify our identity before opening an account. This generally requires us to email off a photo of some government issued ID, like a passport or national identity card, along with a recent bill showing our home address. It's the same sort of thing we expect to do at any decent brokerage, but the difference here is that because literally anyone can set themselves up as a 'bitcoin Exchange', we can't always be sure to whom we are sending our identity. You don't need me to lay out the risks.

One way some popular exchanges try to get around regulation is to provide a number of different account levels, with the lowest level only permitting deposits and withdrawals in cryptocurrencies. If the account is not connected to a commercial bank account, there is no legal requirement for regulation[19]. If we are keeping funds in crypto rather than in a fiat currency, one of these digital-only accounts may suffice.

Before opening an account at any exchange, we should always perform due diligence. We want to know who is

---

19 - Laws can change, and vary between countries and states.

behind the company, their credentials, their backing, the laws they are bound by, and where they are physically located. And of course, we should ask around for honest reviews (not fake reviews put up by affiliates hoping to cash a commission cheque as soon as we sign up through their link) and opinions from active traders. We would also check news sites like Google News and see if our chosen exchange has been the subject of scandal or the recent victim of a hack. In short, we cannot assume that a fancy website is backed by a professional corporation. We want to know where we are sending our money and to whom we are emailing our identities before we part with either.

Examples of well known bitcoin exchanges include Coinbase, Cryptopay, Spectrocoin, and Gemini.[20]

Trading Accounts

The exchanges I listed above offer pure and simple currency exchange in the same way high street forex dealers do for fiat currency. They buy and sell on their own account, hedging their position in the open market. These outfits are aimed at the average consumer and are fine if all we want is to load up a wallet with bitcoin to use as spending money on the internet.

We, however, are traders, and our objectives are a little different. We want to be able to swap one currency for another and back again potentially within minutes and for very low cost. We need tools like live price charts and a way to manage lots of orders. In other words, we need a trading account, not a simple currency exchange account. Fortunately the world of Bitcoin can provide, and there are no shortage of companies ready to furnish us with an active trader account loaded with almost all the bells and whistles we could hope for.

---

20 - Disclaimer: There are not recommendations.

Coinbase operates its own trading subsidiary called GDAX. Other popular trading exchanges include Bitfinex and Kraken.[21]

Bitcoin trading accounts almost always offer free good quality web-based charting, access to the order book, and order management systems that are functional if not quite as fully featured as we would expect from, say, an established stock broker. We'll find Market, Stop, and Limit orders as standard, and we will usually have the option to set expiry times on our orders. However, I've yet to find a broker who offers automatic Stop orders upon a fill, or any kind of automatic trailing Stop. These will no doubt come eventually, and by the time you read this they may already be standard features.

What is rapidly becoming a standard feature is API access. An API is an Application Programming Interface, which we can think of as being like a bunch of sockets we can plug other programs into. Traders are unlikely to use an API directly, but their presence does open the possibility for software vendors like eSignal or MetaTrader to hook their systems up to a bitcoin exchange to offer live charts and trade entry and management.

Derivatives

We cannot end this chapter without mentioning a handful of completely different ways to trade bitcoin, and those are futures, options, and CFDs. Just as there is a derivatives market for commodities like oil, wheat, and gold, and for currencies and stocks, there are bitcoin derivatives arriving on the scene too.

Both the CME and CBOE offer futures contracts for bitcoin, as does recent startup Deribit (who I previously mentioned because of their buggy software, since fixed

---

21 - Disclaimer: These are not recommendations.

— so they say). Deribit also offers bitcoin options trading, if that's your thing.

We can trade cryptocurrency as a CFD through many mainstream brokers. In the UK that means these trades can be performed as spread bets, making profits free of capital gains tax. Right now it's easy to find CFDs for both Bitcoin and Ethereum.

These derivative products, traded on the major exchanges, provide an opportunity for traders who would like to participate in the Bitcoin market from a relatively safe and regulated environment with which they are already familiar.

Coins & Symbols

Bitcoin was the first cryptocurrency, but it is not the only one. More digital tokens are being launched all the time. Most are worthless, but several have gained traction and are viable for trading.

Life would be simple if every new coin chose a unique name, but of course that would be too easy. For various reasons, there exist *forks* of common currencies. A fork happens when the core engineers who maintain the code that runs a cryptocurrency cannot agree on the future of their currency, and different factions implement different changes. For example, we've seen already that Bitcoin is constrained in the number of transactions it can process in a given time period, and that this limit has caused the network to grow slow and for transactions to become expensive. There have been numerous proposals for how to deal with the problem, but because Bitcoin is decentralised and thus has nobody in overall charge, unless there is consensus from everyone using the currency, little can be done. In 2017, one faction of core developers went ahead and made a change to the computer code that makes Bitcoin work. Because not everyone implemented the update, the blockchain — and therefore the currency — was split in two, the original Bitcoin, and a new currency called Bitcoin Cash.

The upshot of forking is twofold. Firstly, we have extra currencies we can trade. Secondly, and more importantly, we should always make sure we know what currency we are dealing with when trading it. It would not pay open a trade in bitcoin then try to close it in bitcoin cash!

Ticker Symbols

As traders, we are used to ticker symbols or abbreviations. Stocks, futures, and currencies are all commonly abbreviated to short three or four letter codes. Cryptocurrencies are also represented by symbols on the exchanges, though not always with the same consistency we have come to expect from the wider trading world.

Bitcoin is decentralised, and although the technical specification that makes it work is fixed in documents and code, anything else surrounding the currency is up for grabs. That includes the symbols used to represent it on the exchanges.

Bitcoin itself is commonly abbreviated to BTC. Confusingly, the popular exchange Kraken uses the BTC symbol in its marketing materials but chooses to use XBT on its trading platform. Monero is another commonly traded coin with a less-than-intuitive symbol — it is usually abbreviated to XMR.

Here are some other common cryptocurrency symbols we are likely to come across on the exchanges:

ETH - Ethereum

ETC - Ethereum Classic (a fork of Ethereum)

LTC - Litecoin

BCH - Bitcoin Cash (a fork of Bitcoin)

BTG - Bitcoin Gold (another fork of Bitcoin)

DASH - Dash

Satoshi & Bits

A single bitcoin is currently worth thousands of dollars. When paying for goods and services, that generally means we aren't sending whole bitcoins but are transacting with fractions of a bitcoin. Probably very small fractions! Rather than discuss fractions, bitcoins are subdivided into smaller units, similarly to how dollars are subdivided into cents, and pounds into pence.

A single bitcoin is divided into one hundred million *satoshi*. So 1 satoshi = 0.00000001 BTC. Although the blockchain itself is actually denominated in satoshi[22], there is no standard currency symbol for satoshi.

In December 2017, another Bitcoin Improvement Proposal, BIP176, suggested that the term *bit* be used to refer to 100 satoshi.

---

22 - Both *satoshi* and *satoshis* are accepted plural terms in the Bitcoin community.

Getting Started

To trade bitcoin, or any other cryptocurrency, we only need a few things: a wallet from which we can transfer funds to and from a trading account, an account at an exchange that is set up for high frequency trading, some price charts, and a decent computer.

It used to be that computers for trading had to be highly specified expensive machines we could dedicate to the task. These days, just about any commodity PC or tablet is up to the job. That said, I always recommend trading from something with a battery — be that a laptop or tablet, or a desktop with an uninterruptible power supply. Getting caught mid-trade by an electrical outage or someone tripping over the mains lead and yanking it out the back of the machine is something best left for others to experience.

Buying and selling cryptocurrencies from a smartphone is possible, and some exchanges even offer apps for this purpose, but those screens are too small for serious trading. We don't need massive multi-monitor set-ups to trade profitably, but we do want to be able to read a chart, see the order book, and view our order tickets all at once. Phones are best kept as backup devices, a means to get out of a trade if all else fails.

For charting, the exchange will provide us with all we need. Most use charts from TradingView.com. At the time of writing, the heavyweight mainstream charting packages like eSignal are not supporting crypto price feeds. Some slightly smaller players like Medved Trader and Updata have integrated one or two exchanges (usually GDAX or Bitfinex), so I expect the bigger outfits to catch up soon.

If you desperately want access to bitcoin trading through your favourite package or broker, there are futures, ETFs, and CFDs.

Wallets are something we've already covered in depth. All I will say on the matter is that we should consider security above all else when choosing a wallet product, and we should also bear in mind that there's no reason to restrict ourselves to a single wallet. A wallet for day-to-day transactions plus cold storage for longer-term securing of funds is a good combination.

Trading Opportunities

Bitcoin is different things to different people. To some it is the currency of the future. To others it's a currency of the here and now, statistically most often used to purchase the sort of thing you don't want your local law enforcement agency finding out about. Some see it as a store of value, a digital alternative to precious metals in which to stash funds safely for the long term. Others regard bitcoin purely as a tradable commodity, just another instrument to be bought and sold for profit.

The multi-faceted nature of Bitcoin and other cryptos opens up some interesting opportunities for traders. We can trade coins much the same way we trade any other currency, but there are unconventional methods to profit from Bitcoin too.

In the next two chapters we will delve into both conventional and unconventional trading methods. We'll cover some overarching principles for trading cryptocurrency, and we will discover which tools in the trader's toolbox can be usefully applied with Bitcoin, and which are best avoided.

Conventional Trading

If you have traded forex before, you will be right at home with bitcoin. It stands to reason — we're using one currency to buy another, it's just that some of the currencies we are open to trading now are not backed by governments or nation states. That detail may sound unimportant, but actually it makes a big difference, primarily because of who trades bitcoin, how they trade it, and in what volumes.

The forex market is vast. Somewhere between three and five *trillion* dollars-worth of currency (estimates vary) is traded around the world every twenty-four hours. Governments, national reserves, central banks, investment banks, commercial banks, and independent traders all participate in this gigantic market, pumping mind-blowing sums of cash through the system. Like an ocean-going super-tanker, the forex market is a huge beast that can be difficult to turn about. This makes for some lovely tradable trends on occasion, and it also makes the market very difficult to manipulate.

Bitcoin is not like traditional forex. Governments, national reserves, and central banks are not (at the time of writing) weighing in, at least not in any serious volume. Some investment banks are dipping their toes in the water, and there are venture backed firms with a few tens of millions of dollars in funding having a play at the edges too, but this is all peanuts compared to the colossus that is forex. Bitcoin is not a super-tanker, it's a yacht bobbing in the ocean of finance. It can shift at speed, but it is volatile and susceptible to being blown off course or caught in a storm. Bitcoin is traded by bit-players (excuse the pun), independents like you and me, and more than a few Chinese miners who are in on the game.

Not only is the number of people trading cryptocurrency far smaller than the number trading traditional forex, the demographic is wildly different too. Most bitcoin traders are not professional traders. In the nicest possible way, they are nerds[23] first, traders second. Bitcoin is a new technology, and like all new technologies it attracts a certain type. The clever sort who love to spend days and nights at their computers, writing code and getting their hands dirty in the nuts and bolts of what makes all this stuff work. Some of them might have experience in finance, perhaps working on banking systems, but their day job is software, not the markets. A percentage of these people will naturally become attracted to the chance to trade this new 'techno-money' for profit.

Then there are those who are not necessarily nerds but who have heard of Bitcoin and have heard it's the new gold rush. They too, lack any practical experience in trading in a professional manner.

This non-pro demographic means a substantial part of the Bitcoin market is inexperienced and unsophisticated. The cryptocurrency market is a kind of kindergarten for traders.

As you might expect, inexperienced traders are looking for obvious signals. Their behaviour is predictable. If they see the price jumping skywards, they have a tendency to jump on board for the ride with little thought of the risks.

The nerd-factor plays into the market in another way. If there's one thing technology types love, it's programming a computer to do their job for them. The Bitcoin world is

---

23 - I don't use the word 'nerd' in a derogatory manner. I have the utmost respect for anyone who can program a computer. They are undoubtedly far more intelligent than myself. The word is a handy shorthand.

filled with clever folks who believe any task can be reduced to an algorithm. Lots of stock, futures, and forex trading is automated of course, and investment banks spend millions on systems that can scalp a fraction of a penny from a trade a microsecond faster than their competitors. Back in Bitcoin land, it's clever boys and girls with regular hardware who are analysing the market and coming up with programs that buy and sell on considerably less sophisticated triggers. Bitcoin, being a purely digital currency traded through exchanges that make it easy for anyone to connect to programmatically, is a magnet for this kind of activity. These amateur-hour trading robots pick up the most obvious signals, adding to the predictability of price in many situations.

Keep It Simple

The most important thing in trading bitcoin is this: get back to basics. Simple setups work great. The more obvious the trading signal, the better. A large proportion of the market are looking for basic trades because it's all they know. The robot-traders are the same, seeking out hard and fast buy and sell signals. Both will take them without a second thought.

My personal trading philosophy has always been to keep it simple; if I can see an entry then so can a thousand other traders. This is even more the case in Bitcoin because those other thousand traders might as well be *all* the people trading at that point in time.

We want to stick to common timeframes, and common indicators if we are going to use them. Most unsophisticated traders take whatever charts their exchange gives them. Only the more adventurous will go fiddling about with the settings. In general that means sticking to 5 minute, 30 minute and 1 hour charts, as well as dailies (bitcoin is not liquid enough for 1 minute charts to be worthwhile). The same thing goes for indicators — accept the defaults. We want to see what the masses are seeing.

I can't emphasise this point enough. Load up a BTC/USD chart and take a look back without touching a single setting. Go on, try it now, I'll wait. Unless today is a strange anomaly, you will see strong support and resistance levels. You'll see long trends interspersed with classic areas of consolidation. You'll see breakouts on volume spikes. Bitcoin charts look like they were drawn by someone who read a textbook description of what a trading chart should look like. You already know how to trade this stuff, so don't overcomplicate it.

Sizing & Margin

Unlike regular currency trading, margins on bitcoin trades are smaller. Much smaller. Two or three times margin is usual. That's less than the typical four times margin stock traders are used to dealing with, and compared to the hundred or more times leverage we can regularly find at a forex exchange, bitcoin seems downright stingy. This has practical effects on how we trade bitcoin. Let's take an example: the price of bitcoin is $10,000 and we risk $100 on a long trade (i.e. we purchase 0.01 BTC for $100). The price moves in our favour by $100 and we sell to take profit. That profit, without margin, is $1. A single dollar for a $100 move in the price. Even at three times margin, we're looking at three bucks.

This means if we want to make serious money from bitcoin, either we will have to put more than $100 on the line for every trade we take, or we are going to have to look for trades where the price moves are expected to be considerably greater. Or both. It's down to the individual trader, of course.

The great thing about trading bitcoin is because there are no minimum account or contract sizes, novice traders, or traders new to this market, can have a go with minimal risk. There's no reason not to throw a hundred bucks into an exchange and have a try. And those with experience and a fund to match can play for the same kind of returns they might see from more conventional markets.

Cryptowat.ch

Before we go any further, I want to introduce you properly to a fantastic website called Cryptowat.ch. It is free to use for all but a handful of features that can be obtained for a modest subscription. Cryptowat.ch is owned by bitcoin exchange Kraken, and if you have an account with Kraken you can connect it to Cryptowat.ch and get some of those extra features for free.

Either way, you can follow along with this book using the free version of Cryptowat.ch.

When we first go to the website, we find a screen that looks something like this (I've inverted the colours here to make it easier to see):

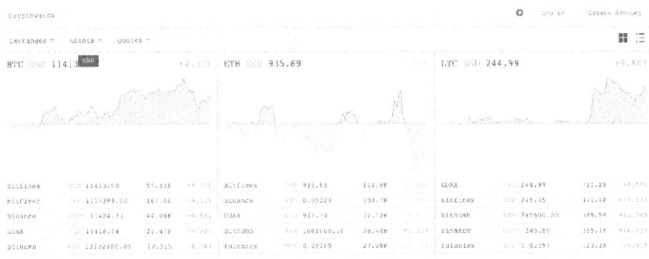

Cryptowat.ch, as the screen shot makes clear, is a kind of price aggregator, bringing together price information from many of the larger exchanges. And not just bitcoin prices, but all the popular cryptocurrencies including Ethereum and Litecoin as shown above. So far so pretty, but things get really interesting when we click on a chart or a price. Then we see something like this:

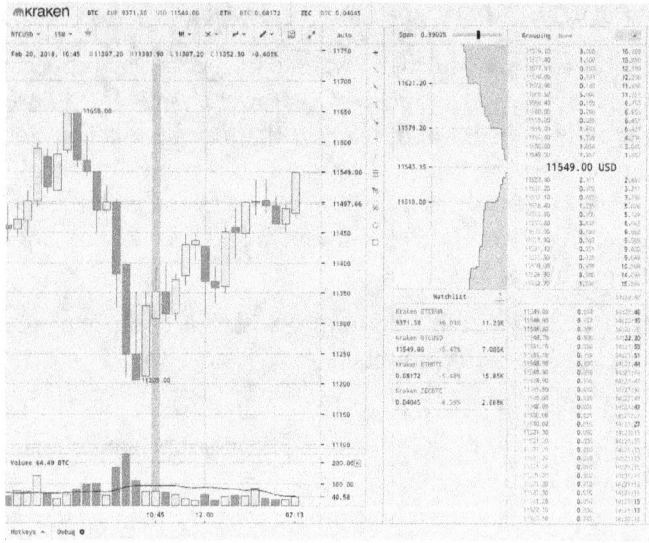

Cryptowat.ch gives us a lovely candlestick chart of the sort we know and love[24]. We also get the order book, the tape, a watchlist, and some spot prices along the top of the screen.

For traders coming from the world of stocks and shares and their expensive data feeds and software, this all looks pretty great. It gets better. If we connect a Kraken account to Cryptowat.ch, we can trade right from the screen above. And Kraken is only one of a number of supported exchanges, there are several more that can be connected.

---

24 - If you are unfamiliar with candlestick charting, there is a primer in Appendix I of this book.

So if we choose to use this site, we can learn one interface to trade from multiple exchanges.

Support, Resistance, And Round Numbers

Enough theory, let's have a proper look at a five-minute BTC/USD chart:

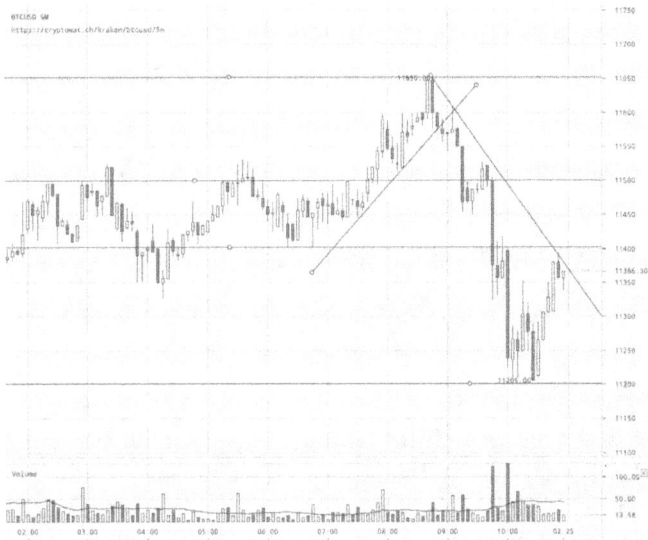

I didn't go hunting through backtest data to find this, I literally took a screenshot of the live chart as I sat down this morning to begin writing this section. I've superimposed a few support and resistance lines as you can see, but honestly, most of those lines are so obvious they don't need to be drawn.

The first thing to note is how the price tends to 'snap' to round numbers (or decade numbers, i.e. numbers ending in zero). Bitcoin traders love round numbers. They love them more than stock traders, and that's saying something. The high on the chart is bang-on a decade number (11,650). 11,500 is extra special because it's a double-zero number, and we can see the price took a couple of attempts to get through it. Same with the next double-zero, 11,600. Triple-zeros are even stronger areas of support and resistance.

When trading bitcoin then, round numbers can be thought of as assumed support/resistance lines, and the more zeros the number ends in, the stronger it is. We should always take note of round numbers when entering trades, thinking of them as a wall we don't want to walk into. Conversely, a bounce from a round number can provide an excellent entry. Round numbers should also be considered when looking for a suitable exit. Every bitcoin strategy needs to take their power into account.

Finally of note on this chart, I added a couple of trend lines. The down-trend line was tested almost right where it met a double-zero number. Good opportunity for a trade!

Zero Bouncing

It is not the aim of this book to teach individual trading strategies, it is my intention to lay out what works and what doesn't in the world of Bitcoin, giving you the trader a shortcut into adapting your own methods for this exciting new opportunity[25]. Having said that, I would like to point out a super-simple scalping opportunity, and a good one for getting your feet wet in the world of Bitcoin. Being a scalping setup, we are not looking for big wins. This is about taking multiple small bites out of the market. With margin and a decent account balance, those can add up quickly to a nice profit.

The zero bouncing strategy is all about leveraging bitcoin's love of round numbers in order to scalp sideways movement. If we look at the early part of the previous chart, we

---

25 - If you are new to trading and don't have any strategies or setups of your own, you can find some starter setups in Appendix 2.

can see the price oscillating between 11,400 and 11,500 for about six hours. It broke through the boundaries a few times, but for the majority of this duration it was ricocheting back and forth. Buying or selling on the double-zero bounces with the next double-zero as a price target is as simple as it gets. Here are some trades we could have taken:

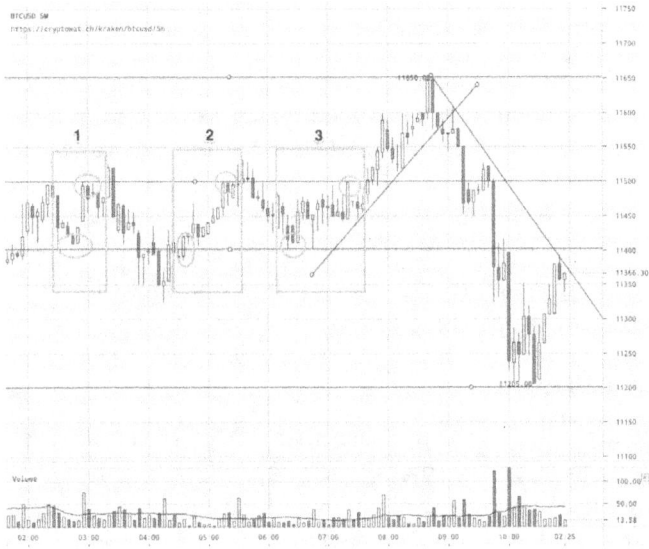

Once the range had been established, there was a nice bounce in box 1, with plenty of opportunity to exit at the target price.

Missed that? No problem. After a brief excursion outside the range, the price came back in again with a strong move upwards. We could have bought on the highlighted bar, or more conservatively on the bounce three bars later.

There was another trade between boxes two and three, but the nicer one is box three on the clean bounce highlighted. Again, plenty of opportunity to get out at the target price.

Sure, trading these would have missed the upswing after box three, but this is a quick in and out scalping strategy, and the two prior trades more than make up for the missed upswing later.

This method doesn't have to be exclusive to double-zero round numbers, it works equally well with regular old single zeros. In some ways it's even easier to trade that way because as we can see from the chart, there are loads of bounces between those decade numbers. Smaller rewards for sure, but smaller risk too.

Zero bouncing is a handy method for profiting from those dull periods when the market is moving sideways. Personally I'm not one for indicators, preferring pure price action, but if you like the crutch of an extra line on your chart, a ten or fourteen period EMA going flat is a good signal that the trend is over for now and that some zero bouncing might be in order.

Volume

Relative to almost any other market, with the possible exception of penny stocks, trade volume in bitcoin is very low, and in all the other cryptos — even the most popular — it's lower still. That makes it especially important to keep an eye on because it doesn't take much to move the price.

Volume spikes often occur at the end of trends, providing a great exit signal. There is an example of a volume spike on the previous chart, marking the end of a $450 price drop that lasted about an hour. We can also see in that chart the volume spike coincided with a double-zero round number. Volume can make an excellent exit confirmation signal.

Order Book & The Tape

Most bitcoin exchanges expose their order book. Stock traders used to a Level 2 screen will be right at home with this market depth data, showing us the Limit orders traders have put in and that have not yet been filled. For forex traders, access to the order book will probably be new.

Here's what the order book looks like on Cryptowat.ch:

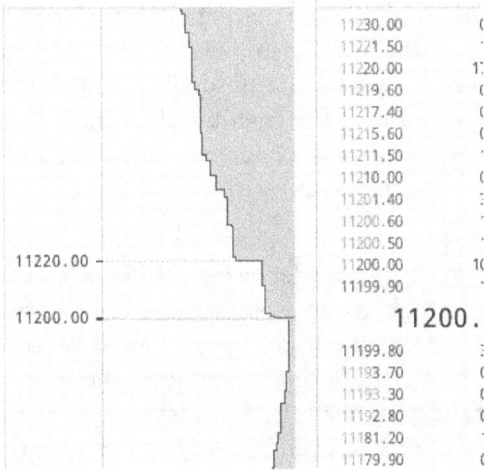

Underneath the order book we have the tape (or the ticker) — in other words live trade data as it happens. Again this will be familiar ground for stock traders.

I'm a huge fan of reading the tape in the stock market because it is unbeatable in giving the trader a feel for where the momentum is. Unlike the order book, which is fluid and capricious, the tape does not lie. It provides us the absolute truth about what is happening *right now* with regard to price.

That's the stock market though, and we're all about bitcoin here. With bitcoin, matters are a little different. Firstly, trading volume is low, so there is far less momentum in the price — certainly not enough to be influencing entry decisions. Secondly, and more importantly, the order books on the bitcoin exchanges are more reliable sources of information than they are in the stock market. Of course, we must always be mindful of the fact that orders on the book can be pulled at any time. There's nothing to stop a player with deep pockets putting in a huge bid in an effort to influence the price, then pull it at the last minute. But bitcoin being a young and unsophisticated market, these sorts of games are rarer than the shenanigans we would see on a NASDAQ Level 2 screen. The bitcoin order book is very much our friend.

Looking at the order book, we see the orders themselves on the right-hand side (showing the bid or ask price, order size, cumulative size, plus the last traded price in the middle), and a graphical representation of cumulative orders on the left. Note the graphic is showing us much more of the book than the few lines of text. The slider at the top of the graphic can be used to zoom in or out to see even more, or to get closer to the detail level on the right. Cryptowat.ch can also display a simplified version of this graphic inside the y-axis scale of the price chart (it's on by default).

If we move our mouse pointer over the order list, the position of those orders is highlighted on the left-hand graphic. And if we move the mouse over the graphic, the price levels are superimposed on the chart. (On a tablet, prodding a finger on the list or the graphic accomplishes the same thing). Important price levels (those where sizeable orders are waiting) are already labelled on the graphic for us.

The order book is a scalper's dream. It makes it easy to see very short term price direction. Looking at the screen shot on page 113, we will note that the price has come up against a lot of sellers at the 11,200 price point — a double-zero number. The thick red wedge of the graphic makes this resistance obvious in comparison to the sliver of green below. It's a no-brainer to go short here, with a tight stop just above that lump of orders at 11,200 in case they get pulled. Here's what happened on the chart in the next few bars after that short was taken:

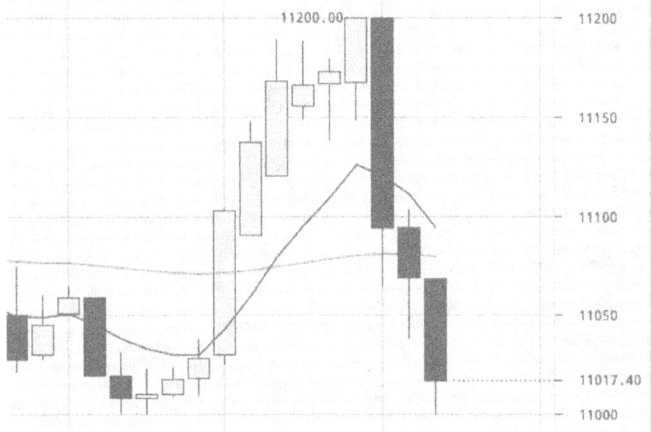

The price dropped away quickly, falling $200 dollars in under fifteen minutes. The triple-zero 11,000 price point was an obvious target, and as we can see from the chart, the price had already bounced from that level not long prior to the move. Note also how the moving averages on this chart would not have helped us get into this trade. Calculated indicators, however complex, all lag (no matter what some people try to claim). They are based on past price action so by definition can only summarise the past. If we were relying on the MAs to show us the way, we would have missed the move. The order book though, is a peek into a possible future. It offers a strong hint about where the price is headed in the short term. Taken together with the double- and triple-zero numbers, we have a good case for a quick short.

Here's another order book screen shot:

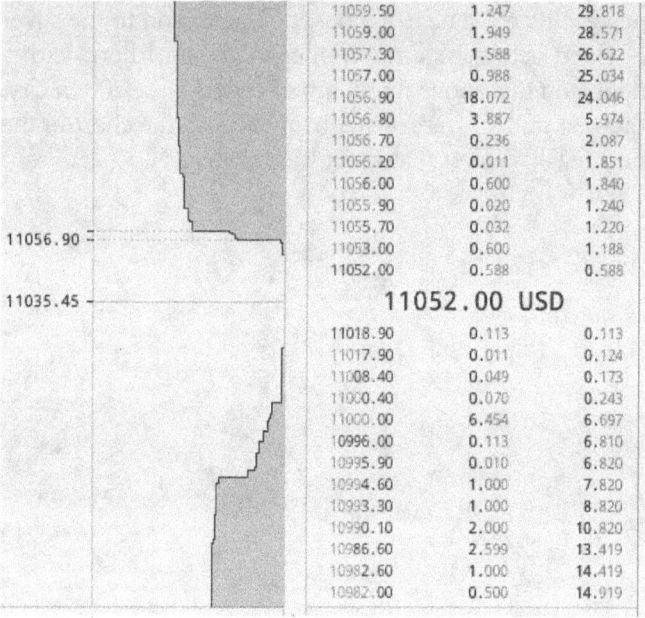

There are a few things of note in this example:

- The bid/ask spread has opened up from the typical $0.10 to a massive $34.00, suggesting a widening difference of opinion on where the price is headed.

- The ask prices are tightly packed. Lots of sellers are ready to offload their bitcoin within a narrow price band, which is also shown graphically with the near horizontal wedge of red. In contrast, the bids are literally few and far between, with sizeable gaps. If those orders are filled, the price will fall precipitously. We can see in the last column that there are cumulatively fewer bids than asks, which is further evidence that in the very short term at least, the price is going down.

- The last trade was at the ask price, so it's not unreasonable to try to stick an order in just under the lowest ask and hope for a fill to go short.

Keeping a close eye on the order book is a step up from the Zero Bouncing strategy presented above. It can help to fine tune entries. We can see support and resistance on the book before it ever shows up on the chart, which means we can avoid walking into a wall. And when we are ready to exit, we can place our order with pinpoint precision to give ourselves the best compromise between a quick fill and a good price.

I highly recommend taking half an hour when you know you won't be disturbed, picking an exchange on Cryptowat.ch, setting it to show BTC/USD, and watching the order book live. You can do this any time of day or night and any day of the week — the market will be there for you. As you observe the book, try to ignore the chart far as possible. Watch the orders as they pop into the list, see how the price reacts to them, how many get filled and how many get pulled, and how the bid and ask pressure pushes and pulls the price up and down. Use the + and - grouping buttons at the top of the order book screen to tighten it up and see more of the book. The longer you spend on this exercise, the better you will feel and understand the bitcoin market.

Timeframes

Bitcoin can be traded on any timeframe we like — in theory. In practice, there are some caveats. I've already alluded to the fact there's not enough volume for super-fast scalping. Quick bitcoin trades tend to last minutes, not seconds.

At the other end of the scale, cryptos can be too unstable for overnight holds. Clearly this is a question of personal preference, but it only takes a major exchange being hacked (which happens with alarming regularity), or the Chinese government to announce restrictions on Bitcoin-related activity, for the price to plunge. Historically the price has usually recovered after such falls, but we all know that past performance is no guarantee of future gains!

Time Periods

In most other markets, even forex, certain periods of the day are more important than others. In the US stock market for example, the range set in the first hour of trading can be very significant, and subsequent breaks of that range provide us with great trade opportunities. In forex, the market open times in the main financial centres of the world are also very important, and entire trading strategies can be built around them.

Similarly, the range set in the previous day's trading is important in many markets. Previous days' open, high, low, and close prices are so significant that most charting packages make it easy to plot them.

Bitcoin is different. Because it truly trades 24/7, there is no market open, no range finding early in the session as overnight sentiment is traded into the price. Sure, technically we can plot a previous day's range on a chart, but it's meaningless. With no major financial centre leading the market, any time period we define as a day is purely arbitrary.

Adapting Strategies

Ultimately, most strategies that are profitable on forex will work well on bitcoin and other cryptos, especially anything that attempts to follow a trend. Momentum plays are out, and obviously so is anything that relies on an open price or a gap, as described above. The same goes for scheduled news — there isn't any that affects cryptos. Simple pattern-based and pure price plays work a treat.

Existing strategies should be pared back to their bare bones where possible. If indicators are used, their values should first be tested using the defaults provided by Cryptowat.ch (the most popular crypto trading platform) and Trading View, whose charts are the default offering for the larger exchanges. Between them, these two platforms have the most traders' eyes. We need to see what the crowd is seeing.

Whatever our method, we must ensure we take account of round numbers, and regard volume with prudence, knowing that it takes very little to have a large effect. Which is why we should also pay close attention to the order book. Its wealth of data, laying bare the intentions of the market, can help us fine tune every entry and every exit, squeezing the maximum profit from each and every trade.

If you don't already have a successful trading strategy of your own to adapt, there are some ideas in Appendix 2 to get you started.

Unconventional Trading

Perhaps Bitcoin's biggest difference over classic markets is the unconventional trading opportunities it throws our way. Unconventional, in the sense I'm using the term here, is anything that isn't simply watching a chart and basing entries and exits off price data. Now that we know how Bitcoin and other cryptocurrencies work on a technical level, we are ready to see how its unique nature opens up these opportunities.

None of the methods described here are recommendations, my job is only to bring them to your attention. Some of them are more accessible than others. As always, it is up to the individual trader to asses every trading opportunity, the risk and reward potential it offers, and to decide whether it's for them.

Arbitrage

Let's get this out right away: bitcoin arbitrage is hard, and it's getting harder. It is already beyond the means of most traders, but I'm including it here because it's often lauded as a great way to profit from bitcoin. Intelligent traders should be aware of the risks involved before jumping in with both feet.

First off, a quick definition so that we're all on the same page. Arbitrage is the practice of profiting from price differentials for the same asset. A glance at our friend Cryptowat.ch will demonstrate the theoretical potential.

We're looking at the BTC/USD price across a number of exchanges. The second exchange on the list, GDAX, is quoting $10,580.48. As we go down the list, most of the other exchanges are pretty close on price...until we get to CEX.IO, who are quoting $10,815.80 — a whopping $235.32 difference.

In theory, we could go and buy $10,580-worth of bitcoin on GDAX, send it to a wallet on CEX.IO, and flog it for a risk-free profit of $235. Do that all day and we'll be rich, right? That's what the arbitrage advocates would have us believe. It's a nice idea, and back in the day it was almost that simple. There are some 'gotchas' though.

The biggest two issues facing anyone attempting bitcoin arbitrage today are transaction times and fees. Back in the day, the sort of move described above was easy to pull off. Transferring bitcoin from one wallet to another cost pennies and could be done in well under an hour. There was always the risk the price moved against you in that time, but it was low. Today, the congested network means fees have skyrocketed and transaction times have slowed to a crawl. It's not unusual for transactions to take twenty-four hours or more to be mined, and to cost high double-figures for the privilege. When we have to spend half or more of that potential $235 profit in fees, all while hoping the price doesn't move against us in the day or so it takes for the bitcoin to get where we need it, the opportunity loses its appeal.

Apart from the fees and timing problem, there is another issue with bitcoin arbitrage. Price differentials of the magnitude we can see above should, in a normal, healthy, functioning marketplace, get traded out in seconds. The market should find equilibrium. The fact these differentials exist are an indicator that something, somewhere is wrong. What happens to be wrong here is the exchange offering the unusually high price is doing so because it does not currently allow account holders to withdraw funds in US dollars, and it needs something to attract trade to make up for that fact. So if we executed our arbitrage trade and were lucky enough that the price did not move in the time it took our bitcoin to arrive at the exchange, then sold it back for dollars, we would be stuck with those dollars until we further traded them for another currency. CEX also happens to charge uncommonly high fees, which if we were not a wary and savvy trader, would further eat into our profit. Given these limitations, it is no wonder CEX is offering a higher price to attract custom. Looking at the volume being traded on the exchange compared to GDAX and Bitfinex, it looks like traders aren't taking the bait.

The final nail in the coffin of arbitrage for the average retail trader comes in the form of the friendly nerd. I've mentioned how cryptos attract a certain type of person — the kind generally more *au fait* with technology than finance. These people have the skills to create automated systems that can seek out and take advantage of arbitrage opportunities in the cryptocurrency market. Such automated systems can monitor the *mempool* in real time and find opportunities when transaction times and fees are low, then pounce. This is one area where the boffins definitely have the upper hand.

All things considered, it is so risky, difficult, and expensive to arbitrage bitcoin that it is not worthy of further consideration as a strategy. We can't beat the boffins at their own game. There are better, safer, and more profitable ways to trade.

Having said that, bitcoin is only one currency. As new cryptos come on stream, or become popular — cryptos that aren't crippled by suffocating fees and transaction times — new arbitrage opportunities can pop into existence.

Talking of new cryptos...

Initial Coin Offerings

Bitcoin hit the news big time in 2017 as it defied expectation and common sense to rise more than 1,300% over the course of the year. But there was another major story in cryptocurrency in 2017, a story that was perhaps less reported but that was every bit as important. It was the story of the Initial Coin Offerings, or ICOs.

ICOs are the cryptocurrency equivalent of IPOs, or Initial Public Offerings. In an IPO, stock in a company is listed on an exchange for the first time, and members of the public are invited to invest in it before it begins trading. In an ICO, a new cryptocurrency is launched, and the public is invited to purchase pre-mined currency before it goes into circulation.

If you are thinking, *"That sounds like a licence to print money,"* then you're right. And if you're thinking, *"Buying new money with real money before that new money has been shown to have any value sounds like a terrible idea,"* you are right again.

ICOs are, almost entirely, a scam. Remember, cryptocurrency is an unregulated market. Literally anyone can invent a new currency, mine it exclusively (and at essentially no cost), then sell it. ICOs usually take the form of a crowdfunding campaign (a bit like a Kickstarter product), inviting 'investors' to get in early with the promise of massive profits when the currency goes live. They tempt the unwary with the true story of how bitcoin was once worth fractions of a cent and now trades for five-figure sums. Their new currency, they claim, will do the same. They are offering a 'once in a lifetime chance' to be in at the start.

Creating new cryptocurrencies used to be a hard, technical challenge, but Ethereum (which can, in simple terms, be used as a sort of building block for making new cryptos) has made it easier, and new toolkits on the market are making it simpler still. An Initial Coin Offering truly is money for nothing, apart from a bit of marketing.

Some ICOs come with promises of greatness, a unique selling point that, their creators say, assure early investors of massive profits because *their* currency is different —

useful in some way. In reality, the only people guaranteed to profit from an ICO are those who are pre-mining and selling the new currency. After that, anything can happen. And what often happens is that the party behind the ICO walks off into the sunset with the fiat currency their investors have plied them with in return for worthless digital tokens, never to be heard from again. Sometimes they stick around for a bit, keep hyping their new token to try to bump the price higher so they can offload even more to the unsuspecting, greedy, and uninformed, before disappearing.

And disappear they do. In 2017 there were at least *nine hundred* ICOs. In that same year, according to a survey[26], almost half of those new currencies 'failed' — by which I mean their creators took the real money invested and disappeared. $104 million of fiat currency went with them. Even more are at death's door, as good as failed. Perhaps the lesson here is that if you want to get rich quickly, invent a cryptocurrency!

That still leaves 54% of the ICOs alive and kicking though, so is there something to all this? Yes and no. Supposedly reputable companies are getting in on the game, launching specialist currencies and other blockchain-based products. The problem is a lot of them are doing so because 'blockchain' is the buzzword *du jour* and getting in on the blockchain act is a surefire way to attract venture capital.

So the real lesson here is to be aware of what ICOs are, and to treat them with extreme caution. As with everything, it's down to the individual investor whether they want to get involved. Assume every ICO is a scam from the start, and perform due diligence to prove otherwise beyond all reasonable doubt. If it can't be proven, steer clear.

---

26 - Survey data: https://news.bitcoin.com/46-last-years-icos-failed-already/

Leading Exchanges

Earlier we saw how Bitcoin's decentralised nature and variety of exchanges can create arbitrage opportunities. And we saw how profiting from those opportunities is far from child's play. But the plethora of exchanges does open the door to another play that is almost unique to the world of cryptocurrency. That play is simply this: some exchanges lead others. To understand why that is, let's have another look at that Cryptowat.ch screenshot from earlier in the book.

Rather than focus on the price this time, we need to concentrate on the volume traded on the exchanges. It's clear Bitfinex is the big daddy here. At the time that image was taken it had traded more than 32k on the day. The next biggest volume was less than half that at a little over 14k, and the third exchange by volume was almost half again, at 8k and change. What this means in practice is Bitfinex has more sway in the market. Every exchange will find its own price as a function of its participating traders, of course, but if the price on the biggest exchange shoots up on substantial volume, sooner or later the traders on other exchanges are going to notice, and they will follow suit. It is simply unsustainable in a functioning marketplace for two exchanges to differ wildly on price *direction* for long, even if their final price is consistently different.

What does that mean for us as traders? It means we can use one exchange as a true leading indicator for another.

Now let's be clear here, when I say one exchange leads another, I'm talking about over a timeframe of under a minute. We can't see it on a chart, it happens too fast for that. But it does not happen so quickly that we can't use it.

We can see this leading action play out by opening two charts on Cryptowat.ch. Patience is required, but we're traders so we are used to that. Ensure both charts are showing the same timescale — personally I like 5 minute charts — sit back, and watch, paying close attention to the direction of the price rather than the price itself. When a sizeable move happens ($50 or more on BTC/USD), it will almost always happen on the bigger exchange first.

If we are to use this information to trade, we will want confirmation from another signal. Price moving on one exchange does not tell us how far that move will go. A leading exchange is not so much a trading method in itself, rather it is is a great confirmation indicator to use with an existing system, in the same way stock traders often use the futures as a leading indicator.

That said, if we are lucky then we can sometimes catch a stellar move on massive volume precious seconds before that same move follows on our smaller exchange. I've personally done this, it works, but it is rarer.

Now for some caveats. First off, we should note that though today Bitfinex is the largest exchange by volume on Cryptowat.ch, tomorrow that could change. As savvy traders it is our job to follow the market closely and ensure we are on top of where the big money is flowing.

Secondly, and perhaps somewhat obviously, like everything in trading we cannot expect this to work all the time — nothing in a free market does. As long as it works more often than it doesn't, it is a useful strategy.

Third, if we watch a larger exchange to predict movements in a smaller one, and we go ahead and trade those moves on the smaller exchange, we will need to be ready to accept the price whipping around on our lower volume exchange. It is only normal that price chops on low volume.

Fourth, it is entirely possible for the smaller exchange to lead the larger one. This doesn't happen a lot, but it does happen. The clue is always in the volume. A huge spike in volume on any exchange is a big flag to watch the other exchanges.

One last observation I will make is that the lower down the list of exchanges we go, the greater the tendency for those exchanges to ignore the bigger players. In other words if we choose to trade on a very low volume exchange, we'll need to see a wider swing in price on the leading exchange before our small exchange takes notice.

Funding Margin

Any bitcoin exchange worth its salt will offer margin trading. They will lend the trader money with which to augment their buying or selling power. That money has to come from somewhere, and because the folks who run the exchanges are generally a smart bunch, they figured out how to access margin funds without putting up their own cash. They take it from other traders. The other traders are willing participants in this scheme, and we can be too. Why would we want to risk our hard-earned cash for someone else to trade with? Because as long as they are using it, they are paying interest on it. If you've ever wanted to be a loan shark but didn't want to put in the effort, now's your chance.

Funding margin is definitely not a get rich quick scheme. Interest rates are in the tenths or hundredths of a percent, but these are daily rates and over time it all adds up. It is certainly possible to achieve a 10% equivalent yearly rate or more, and in this day and age no bank is going to give us anything close to that kind of return. If we have money sitting in a trading account not being actively traded, there is little additional risk in lending it out as margin (the existing risk being that the exchange is hacked or disappears without a trace). Exchanges will liquidate losing positions to recover funds before margin losses occur.

How margin lending is managed depends on the exchange, and is generally a painless process that involves deciding how much of our account balance we are willing to lend, for how long, and in some cases at what interest rate; while some exchanges fix the rate, others let the trader set it in a kind of auction. Exchanges publish their rates along with how much margin is available and how much is in play, which helps us decide where to allocate our funds. Just because we put our cash up as available for lending, doesn't mean it will be lent. We will want to fund a currency that is in demand, and if possible set an interest rate that is both attractive to the borrower and usefully profitable for ourselves.

Because we can fund margin in any currency the exchange supports, we can combine margin funding with a trade. For example, if we are going long bitcoin and are planning on being in for a day or more, we could try to lend that bitcoin position out as margin, earning us some extra on top of any profit the trade generates. When we sell it back for dollars, pounds, or euros (or any other currency), we can lend *that* out too. Our account balance can work for us all the time. Naturally we will have to bear in mind any funds loaned out cannot be used to buy or sell back a position as long as the loan is in force. If the funds we are loaning are the result of a trade and that trade goes against us, we won't be able to close it out until the loan is repaid. Trading is always about managing risk.

Local Bitcoins

Most bitcoin exchanges work in one of two ways: either we buy from and sell to the exchange directly, or they enable our transactions with other market participants. In both cases we have no choice over who takes the other side of our trade. Localbitcoins.com is different. It's a peer-to-peer cryptocurrency exchange. In other words, the website is a free market enabler, bringing together buyers and sellers from around the world. We can think of it simplistically as being the eBay or Craigslist of Bitcoin.

Localbitcoins.com has, like most Bitcoin-related businesses, trodden a rocky path over its short history. It was created in 2012, and within three years it had been hacked once (the loss was small at just $15,000), been excluded from two markets (Germany, and New York State in the US) due to licensing issues, and seen several of its customers charged with money laundering. Yet in late 2017 it had to suspend new account creations temporarily as it was having trouble coping with a massive influx of new customers when the price of bitcoin soared.

The site enables bitcoin trade either physically in person, or online — it's up to the participants how they want to do the deal. Trading bitcoin in person is obviously very risky and I would not advise it; there's too much that can go wrong. Online trade on the other hand, is protected through escrow by default. Combined with a feedback and rating system of the sort any eBay customer will be familiar with, the risk of peer-to-peer transactions can be brought into check.

For traders, the appeal of LocalBitcoins.com lays in the arbitrage opportunities it offers. Let's take a look:

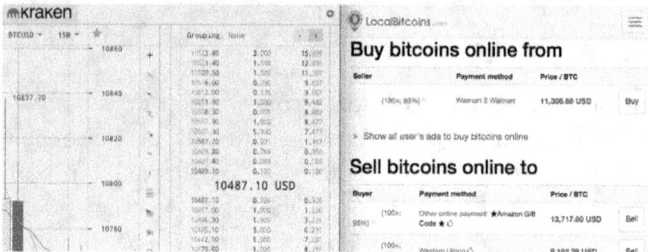

On the left of the screenshot is the bitcoin price at the Kraken exchange. On the right is an ad from a US-based trader on Localbitcoins.com at the same moment in time. The seller (whose name I have removed) is offering to sell bitcoin at about $800 above the current market price. They are accepting payment through the Walmart 2 Walmart payment system. Localbitcoins.com accepts about sixty different payment methods, including PayPal and bank transfer, and prices offered vary according to the risk associated with each method. Bitcoin transactions are irreversible; PayPal transactions are not.

You may be wondering why anyone would pay $800 above the market rate for bitcoin. The answer is that not everyone who wants access to bitcoin has access to more common channels for purchasing it. As traders it's easy for us to forget that not everybody in the world has a bank account or a credit card. For those without, Localbitcoins.com offers an alternative means of obtaining cryptocurrency.

Another reason is that some buyers of bitcoin would like to remain anonymous (we can guess at the many reasons why). To a buyer wishing to keep their identity secret, a regular exchange bound by "Know Your Customer" rules is not an option. Walking into a high street store, buying a gift card with cash, then using that card to purchase bitcoin is a much better solution, and one for which the buyer will be willing to pay a premium.

As we can see from the screenshot, the trader is also happy to *buy* bitcoin — at well below the market rate. Again, though this seems counter-intuitive, there are sellers out there for whom the channels offering the market price are not available, not desirable, or both.

It costs nothing to create an account at Localbitcoins.com, they make their money through a 1% fee charged to advertisers on transactions. While the financial cost of arbitrage on the site may be negligible, there is a significant time cost, especially when getting started. As with any peer-to-peer marketplace, reputation is everything. Even with payments protected by escrow, it takes a brave person to carry out transactions of any decent size with a new advertiser who has no history. Not only does every advertisement display the trader's overall feedback score prominently (93% for the trader in the screenshot, for example), it also reports the total number of confirmed trades (along with the number of different accounts those trades were with), the time the account has been active, how much verification the account holder has provided (a verified email address is mandatory, a phone number advised, and full proof of identity by way of government issued ID is also possible), how many people have marked the account as trusted, and how many have blocked it. Also shown is how long ago the trader was last logged in and active. Combined, this data can provide a high degree of confidence to anyone hoping to trade. If we are looking to transact with an advertiser, we will want to see positive scores across the board. If we want to set ourselves up as an advertiser, buying and selling for a profit, we'll have to work hard at getting those great scores, and we will need to be very active and responsive on the site. Advertisers who respond to trade requests in under five minutes earn a green dot next to their name.

Localbitcoins.com is not for everyone. But it is a great example of the unique trading opportunities this new form of currency brings to the market.

Beware The Pump & Dump

Bitcoin's dearth of regulation, the relative difficulty of linking funds to an individual, the technical nature of the currency, a widespread lack of knowledge among the public, and the massive hype surrounding it, make for a truly toxic combination; Bitcoin attracts scammers. It's easy for the morally dubious and technically savvy to wow the uninitiated with promises of great profits from this amazing new thing they keep hearing about in the news. Even those of us who have a better understanding of what's what can be caught out by genuine sounding schemes if we don't keep our wits about us.

Initial Coin Offerings, or ICOs, as we saw in the last chapter, are probably the favourite method for separating people from their wealth when it comes to cryptocurrency scams. It seems not a week goes by without another ICO being announced, and another ICO 'failing' as the press like to put it, when by failing they mean the organiser waltzing off with all the money investors have put into the thing.

But ICOs are not the only game in town when talking about relieving the naïve profit-seeker of their cash.

Pump and dump schemes are well known to most investors, even though they are illegal in regulated markets. A pump and dump is a pretty simple kind of fraud, which involves the scammer *pumping* up the price of a security — usually a penny stock — by inciting others to purchase it, and *dumping* their holdings to those investors at prices that have become artificially inflated by all the buying activity. Penny stocks have traditionally been the vehicle of choice because they are illiquid, meaning it doesn't take much trading volume to get the price to move, and because they can be found on smaller exchanges where it's easier to game the system without getting caught.

Easier still are cryptocurrencies. Particularly the lesser known ones. As we've already seen, outside of the main tokens like Bitcoin, Ethereum, and Monero, volume on cryptos is very, very thin. And we have noted that most investors in the crypto market are unsophisticated in the sense they have little practical experience of trading or investing. They also tend to be very comfortable with use of the internet, which means they have no fear of forums and chat rooms. They are, in other words, easy prey for pump and dump scammers.

Here's how a pump and dump works *in theory*. This is how it is sold to the unwary investor. The organiser of a pump and dump group will invite investors into their group, usually for a fee to be paid in bitcoin. The group operates a chat room, and payment gets the investor access. On a given date, the organiser will announce to all members the name of the exchange that the next pump and dump will operate on. Obviously for the price to be most affected by mass buying, that buying should all take place on the same exchange. The members will create accounts on the exchange and load them up with funds. At a pre-determined time, the organiser will announce the currency chosen to be pumped, live in the chat room. At that instant, the paid members will start buying as much as they can of the obscure digital token. The price will rise as a result of the buying. At this point the members will usually encourage outsiders to buy too, and this is when they begin dumping their holdings on the new entrants, getting out as the price rises for a healthy profit. As the mass selling ensues, the price drops, and the unsuspecting most recent entrants are left sitting on an equally hefty loss. These poor souls are called *bag holders*. Sounds great if you're a paid member, right? Can't go wrong. So what's to be worried about?

Turns out, things aren't quite what they seem.

The first thing we should note is that not all pump and dump group members are equal. There are multiple layers or levels. Those who pay more for entry are closer to the centre of the group. They get the all important name of the chosen currency a few seconds before those who pay a bit less, which means they get to buy at a better price than those on the outer levels. How many levels exist depends on the group.

Okay, so it seems like pumping and dumping is a great way to make a profit provided we get to join the inner circle. We can dump our holdings on the outer layers, guaranteeing our profits, can't we?

Not so fast. This sort of thinking is what the organisers want from us. In reality, the real pump started long before any paid member was clued in to the name of the chosen currency. The organiser will already have loaded up their own account days or weeks in advance, buying slowly over a long time so as not to move the price in an obvious way. As soon as the paid members start pushing the price upwards, the organiser starts selling, locking in huge profits. Sure, some of the paid members might get lucky and get in and out before the price crashes, but the whole point is guaranteed profits, not getting lucky. Paid members have almost as much chance of ending up as bag holders as those on the outside.

The only person guaranteed to profit from a pump and dump then, is the organiser, and they get to make their money twice. Once from their pre-pumping and subsequent dumping on their unsuspecting members, and a second time from the fees those members are paying them for the privilege.

A variation of this classic fraud is the celebrity pump and dump, where rather than having rafts of paid members incite others to buy (and thus become bag holders), a 'celebrity' — somebody with a sizeable social media following — does the pumping. This is usually a Twitter personality of low morals, someone with a lot of followers who, for a fee, will happily attempt to persuade them to get in on this great cryptocurrency because the price is about to rocket. The sad thing is these poor bag holders will see the price did indeed go up — right as they were buying. Many of them will never suspect they have been duped. The advice was correct, after all, the price did increase. They will just assume they timed their exit badly and that their loss is their own fault. Which means they will be easy to fool the next time around, too.

Pump and dumps occur almost exclusively on smaller exchanges and with smaller currencies. As serious traders working with serious exchanges and trading the main cryptos, we should never find ourselves caught up in one. Usual common sense rules apply: if it sounds too good to be true, it is.

Bitcoin As A Useful Currency

Bitcoin was conceived primarily as a currency, not a trading vehicle or an object of speculation, even if that is what it has become. As a currency, it has mostly failed. High transaction fees, slow confirmation times, the relative complexity of creating and funding a wallet, and exceptional volatility have all conspired to render it undesirable for making regular purchases.

The number of vendors accepting bitcoin as payment for goods or services has dwindled. Nobody wants to amass a currency they can't spend freely, so vendors who do accept it generally want to 'cash out' to fiat currency as soon as the transaction is complete. Given the price could have halved between a sale being made and cashing out, it's not surprising most are unwilling to take the risk. This has created a vicious circle — the fewer merchants there are who accept bitcoin, the less useful it becomes, and the harder it is to persuade new merchants to sign up to it.

That said, there remain a number of businesses who accept bitcoin, including some big names like Expedia, Overstock, and Microsoft, as well as any store hosted on the Shopify network that has elected to accept bitcoin via Bitpay.

Away from these merchants, there are still some ways and means of spending bitcoin, and reasons we may want to do so.

Purse.io

Purse.io enables us to spend bitcoin in the world's biggest store — Amazon. Even better, it lets us buy almost anything from that store at a discounted price.

Purse brings together those who wish to shop on Amazon and pay with bitcoin, with people who would like to obtain bitcoin but who can't or don't want to go through the traditional exchanges.

There are a couple of ways to use Purse.io, but the best is the "Name Your Discount" option. It's very simple. First, we create a buyer account on Purse.io and deposit bitcoin into the wallet that comes with the account. Then we go shopping on Amazon. When we find what we want to buy, we add it to a public Amazon Wish List, paste the URL of that Wish List into Purse, and then decide how much we want to pay for the item or items. We can set our price in good old pounds, dollars, or euros. What's important here is that we can set a price below that being advertised by Amazon. Typically we will go anywhere from 5% to 15% lower. Let's say we're after a TV that normally costs $500. We could pick a price of $450 to get a 10% discount.

Purse takes $450-worth of bitcoin from our wallet, puts it in escrow, then posts our purchase request to their website, to be browsed by people who wish to get hold of bitcoin by non-traditional means. When someone comes along who happens to be looking for about $450-worth of bitcoin, and who is willing to pay $50 to get it, they will take our Purse order, go to Amazon, and buy the TV for us as a gift item. They don't get to see our name or address (though they can see the town the item will be delivered to), Amazon handles that side of things through their Wish List system. Likewise, we don't get to see who purchased the item for us, only their Purse.io username.

When our TV is delivered we notify Purse who release the escrowed bitcoin to the buyer. They get their bitcoin, and we get a discount. We also get an Amazon order number so we have the same level of guarantee and after sales service we would enjoy had we purchased the item ourselves.

Just how much discount we can achieve depends on how long we are willing to wait for someone to buy our item, what our rating is on Purse, and how many bitcoin buyers are active at any given time. Personally I've always found orders with a discount of up to 10% to be filled within a day, 15% within 24 hours, and 20% within 48 hours.

Purse.io takes a commission on every transaction, but the discount we can achieve more than makes up for it.

Pre-Paid Visa & Mastercard

Prepaid Visa and Mastercard debit cards, funded from a Bitcoin wallet, are a way of spending bitcoin anywhere regular credit and debit cards are accepted. There are no shortage of providers who will link a Bitcoin wallet (hosted by them) to a Visa or Mastercard, both of the physical plastic variety and also the newer virtual card (just a card number, delivered electronically), which can only be used online. Virtual cards are usually cheaper and sometimes free, but they also come with tighter funding and spending limits. Examples of providers offering these cards include Cryptopay, SpectroCoin, and Bitpay, but there are many others.

It used to be the case that prepaid cards could be obtained without any form of identity verification, making them a viable option for those wishing to spend bitcoin anonymously. However, recent rule crackdowns by both Visa and Mastercard have pretty much put an end to that, and reputable card providers now require that government issued ID, such as a passport or driving licence, is provided before a card can be issued.

Gift Cards

As pre-paid debit cards become harder to get hold of, gift cards are becoming a more attractive means for spending bitcoin. They are easy to acquire, can be supplied in virtually any denomination, and can be bought entirely online as digital cards which are delivered as a number to be redeemed at a store's website. Gift cards come with the advantage that vendors often run promotions offering extra credit — essentially free money. The downside of course, is that not all stores offer gift cards.

Gyft and eGifter are two big names in digital gift cards, while Giftoff.com has a strong offering for vendors in the UK and Europe. Payment via bitcoin is quick and easy, and cards are delivered by email once the bitcoin transaction has a number of confirmations.

Final Thoughts

Before ending this book, I want to leave you with a few final thoughts about trading cryptocurrency.

We Are Always In A Position

When trading any kind of currency, including cryptocurrency, we are always in a position, even when we are not. All we are doing when trading bitcoin is exchanging one currency for another. Whatever currency we currently hold is our position. If we hold US dollars it should be either because we are not going to be trading them, or because we are lending them as margin, or because we think the price of bitcoin (or whatever we are trading) will diminish in relation to the US dollar. We are never 'out' of the market as long as we have funds in a trading account.

Scammers Are Everywhere

Journalists love to refer to cryptocurrency as the wild west of finance and technology, and they're not wrong. It has been a common theme in this book, and yes, I'm going to say it again. There are scammers, hackers, and charlatans everywhere. I'm not making this up to scare you, it's the reality of working in an unregulated market. If someone steals our coin, we won't get it back. Law enforcement won't be interested, and even if they were, they couldn't do much about it. And even if they *could*, they could just as easily take our money. Think I'm talking from my behind? Two of the FBI officers involved in taking down the notorious darknet drugs market Silkroad were later found to have siphoned off almost a million dollars-worth of seized funds for themselves (bitcoin that is worth considerably more today). Sadly, the rule is: trust nobody.

So Are Amateurs

Even those with honest intentions find themselves caught out when bugs turn up in their software (eg: Deribit). How they handle such issues is out of our control. No regulator will step in, no state-backed insurance fund will save us. Unfortunately the 'socialising' of bitcoin losses is common. We are expected to help pay for the mistakes of others.

Control Your Own Wallet

Given the abundance of scammers, hackers, and the downright incompetent, it makes no sense to keep large sums of bitcoin in a wallet controlled by a third party. Obviously if we are trading on an exchange, we're going to have to keep a float of funds there, but when the profits start rolling in, it is logical to withdraw them to the relative safety of a private wallet as soon as possible. Preferably cold storage.

Stay Informed

More than any other financial product, cryptocurrency is fast moving and fast evolving. Just in the last few weeks of writing this book, news of child pornography in the blockchain has broken, countless ICOs have launched, countless more have 'failed', bitcoin ETFs have become a reality, Google and Twitter have banned Bitcoin related advertising, a US city has banned bitcoin mining, and at least two exchanges have been hacked. And those are only the main headlines. Suffice it to say, if we are active in cryptocurrencies, we should commit to staying on top of the news. Not only can if affect the value of our holdings, it could affect our ability to hold bitcoin at all.

Appendix I - Technical Analysis Primer

Technical analysis is the study of price charts with the goal of trying to predict where price will move in the future. If you're not already familiar with reading price charts, this section will give you a high-level overview. I must emphasise that this book is aimed at those who already have experience of trading, and this appendix is not a substitute for real world experience or more comprehensive training. There are plenty of books on the market that go into much greater depth (including my own). That said, if you are eager to get going, then this section will at least provide you with enough information to understand what's going on in a bitcoin price chart.

The information in this appendix is a heavily abridged and adapted version of the technical analysis chapter from my book *How To Day Trade Forex For Profit*. Naturally I recommend reading that book if you have an interest in currency trading but no prior experience. It goes into much more detail, includes more examples and patterns, and covers charting indicators and how to build strategies based on them.

Price

Prices have a habit of moving in patterns than can and do repeat themselves. Virtually all prices are like this, whether they are for cars, cotton, or currency. Why do prices move in patterns? Because they are set by people, and people are creatures of habit. Technical analysis is the study of prices from the past in an effort to predict those that may occur in the future.

Patterns in prices occur in any timeframe. Markets have a tendency to rise over the long term, with prices increasing until they reach heights that are unsustainable. At that point the bubble bursts, prices fall, and there is a period of consolidation. The boom-and-bust bubble pattern occurs over years or even decades, and has repeated itself for centuries.

Price patterns are fractal in nature, so we find them occurring over much shorter timescales too. We can see the same kinds of patterns lasting months, weeks, days, hours, or even minutes. Why is that so? Again, because prices are made by people, and people have different outlooks ranging from the very short term to the very long term, and everything in between.

There is another reason price patterns repeat, and that is because of self-fulfilling prophecy. If enough people believe that when a price behaves in a certain way then it will do something or other, and if enough of those people take trades according to that belief, they can actually cause the price to do the "something or other" they were expecting.

Price Charts

Charts are our main tool when it comes to technical analysis. They are a graphical summary of price over a fixed period of time. Anything that has a price can be charted. You could chart car prices, candy prices, and as we well know, bitcoin prices.

Charts make it very easy to spot the kinds of patterns that occur in price movements. Consider this sequence of prices, then look at the chart :

```
1.29, 1.29, 1.30, 1.31, 1.32, 1.31, 1.30,
1.29, 1.31, 1.32, 1.31, 1.29, 1.31, 1.32,
      1.32, 1.31, 1.30, 1.29
```

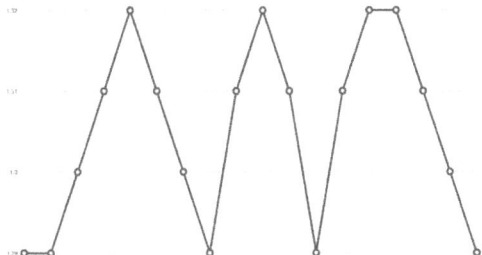

The repeating up-down pattern is easy enough to see, even just reading the numbers. But it's even easier to spot in the chart. This is a simple example with a handful of prices. When we're looking back over more data, charts become invaluable.

If you've already looked at a cryptocurrency chart, or any kind of currency chart for that matter, you will notice that it looks nothing like the line chart in the example above. There's a good reason why. In the prior example, we have sampled the price every few minutes, plotted it on the chart, and connected the dots with a line. The more times the price can be sampled and added to the chart, the more accurate it becomes. But there's a limit to how many points we can physically fit into a line chart like this before it becomes unreadable. Obviously we don't want to leave any price data out, it's all equally important, so rather than plot every single price in a line, we summarise the information.

Bar Charts

We can fit much more price information onto a chart by plotting it as bars. These are the staple of technical analysis, and are used the world over by traders of not just currencies, but also stocks, futures, bonds, options, and commodities. Bar charts look confusing at first, but actually they are really simple. Let's look at how a single bar is constructed. First, we will take a sequence of prices that occurred over a one minute period.

```
0.7660 0.7650 0.7645 0.7655 0.7660 0.7665
       0.7680 0.7675 0.7670 0.7665
```

This is what these prices look like as a classic line chart.

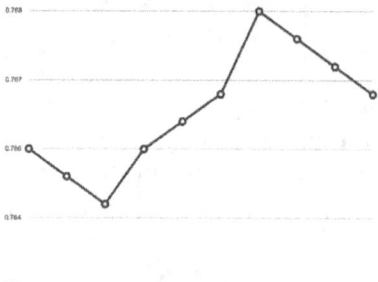

We can summarise the important part of that set of data into a single bar that looks like this:

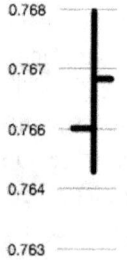

The bar, like a line chart, is read from left to right. The leftmost extremity tells us the price at the start of the bar, in this case 0.7660. The rightmost extremity tells us the price at the end of the bar, which was 0.7665. All the action in between has literally been squashed up into one vertical line. That means the line shows us the range the price travelled in, the highest point it reached being 0.768 and the lowest point being 0.7645.

These price changes could have occurred over any length of time. They might have happened during 10 seconds, 10 minutes, 10 hours, or even 10 years. It doesn't matter how long a time period is represented, the bar will never take up more horizontal space. That means we can represent the full range of prices on a chart without the chart growing to gargantuan proportions horizontally.

A bar then, covers all the prices that occurred during a fixed period of time. It shows us the price at the start and end of the period (we call these the open price and the close price), as well as the highest and lowest prices reached during the period (which we call simply the high and the low.)

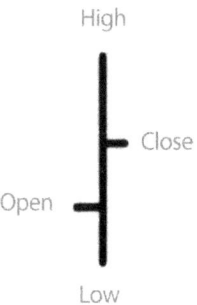

Although this bar contains all the prices covered in time period, we can only be sure about the order in which two of them occurred — the open and the close. We know the price at the close was higher than the price at the open. We also know that at some point during that minute it was higher still, and that at some other point, it was lower than at the open. What the bar doesn't tell us is in what order these price changes happened. In other words, the bar above could have been formed from the sequence of numbers we looked at earlier, like this:

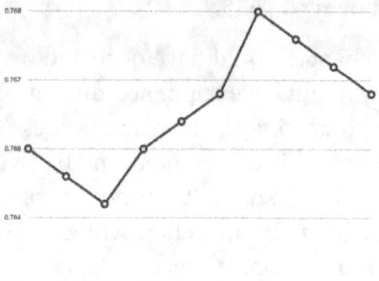

Or it could have formed quite differently, in fact, any of these sequences might have made that bar:

It's important not to make too many assumptions about what a bar is showing us. Bars in isolation give us useful information, but when we start looking at sequences of bars we can learn a lot more.

Bars In Context

As soon as we start putting bars together, we can begin to see patterns emerging, and we can start to form an educated guess about where the price might be headed next. Not many conclusions can be drawn from our previous solitary bar. We know that over the one minute time period it summarises, the price ended up slightly higher than at the beginning, but on its own that information isn't very useful. What about if our bar was the third in this sequence of three bars?

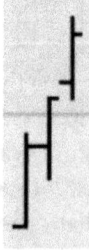

The preceding two bars both closed higher than they opened, as did our bar. There's a *trend* here, the price in this chart is rising. If this was all the information we had to go on, it would be reasonable to guess that in the next bar the price will rise even higher. Of course it would be just that — a guess. It's entirely possible that on the next bar the price drops, or even stays the same. But the fact the price has been rising until this point gives us a hint it may continue to do so.

As traders, our job is to gather hints like this in order to make an informed opinion as to where the price might go next. The more hints that point to the same thing, the greater the probability of that thing being right. We'll never be right in our opinion all the time, but we don't have to be to make a profit.

Candlesticks

Candlesticks are an alternative way of presenting the same information shown in bar charts. Some people find them easier to read, others prefer the simplicity of bar charts.

A candlestick has three components: the thick body of the candle shows the open and close prices for the period covered. The thin wick protruding from the top extends to the highest price reached, and the thin tail sticking out the bottom extends to the lowest price. Here's what our example bar looks like as a candlestick.

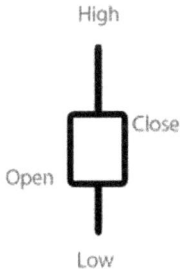

The same four data points are displayed slightly differently. But there's a problem. How do we know if the open was higher than the close? With the bar, the open is always on the left and the close is always on the right, so we know which was which regardless of which was higher or lower. With the candle, the top and bottom of the body represent the open and close, there is no left and right. So how can we tell which is which? Simple — if the body of the candle is empty, as with the candle above, then the open is at the bottom and the close is at the top. The price rose over the time the candle was formed. If the candle body is filled in, then the open was at the top and the close at the bottom. On the right is a candlestick where the price fell.

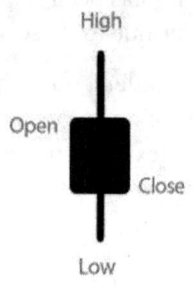

An alternative way of displaying direction in candles is to fill the body with green if the price rose, and red if the price fell.

Here are some chart segments showing the same data as a bar chart and a candlestick chart:

Candlestick charts can be slightly misleading in that the wider body of the candle draws the attention of the eye away from the wick. When we glance at a candlestick chart, it's very easy to give more weight to the range shown by the body (i.e. the range between just the open and close prices), and discount the range of the wick. The solidity of the candle's body makes it appear more important than the thin wick above and below. But the range indicated by the wick is actually more important because that's the full range the price covered during the period of the candlestick.

Support & Resistance

Now we know what a chart looks like, and how the bars or candles that go onto it are made, we can start to look for patterns in those bars. We will start by looking at support and resistance, which form the basis of many (but not all) patterns.

Here is a chart segment. I've left the scale off because it's not important.

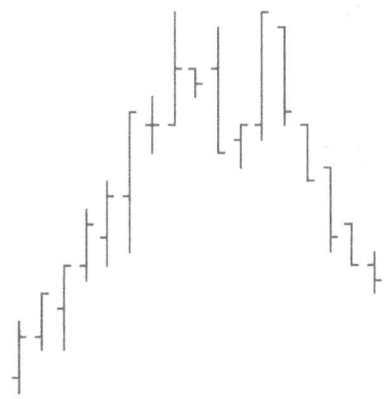

To begin with, the price is rising. Eventually it stops and falls back down a bit. Then it goes back up, gets to pretty much where it managed before, then falls down again. It's almost like it has hit some kind of ceiling. We call this imagined ceiling *resistance*.

We can draw the resistance on the chart.

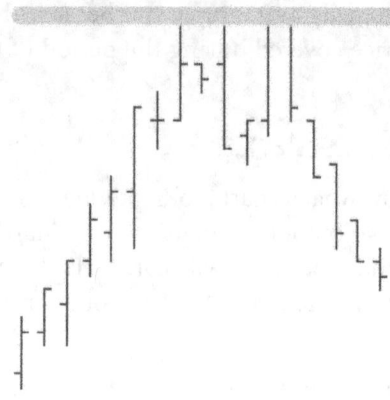

What's going on here? Obviously there is no actual ceiling stopping the price from going any higher, so why is it behaving as if there was? To begin to understand, we need to remember that the chart is showing us price, and that price is a perception of value as viewed by the majority within the market. So we're looking at a graph illustrating the thoughts of a crowd of people. For the first seven bars, the perception of value is gradually rising. People are buying whatever it is we are charting. On the eighth bar something changes, the price stops going up. The price has risen to a tipping point. The majority view has changed. The largest part of the crowd has spoken, and they have said "Enough!" They've stopped buying, which means the price can't get any higher. Either they don't think whatever they are buying is worth any more, or they don't believe it will be worth more in the future, or both.

With not enough buyers around to enable them to raise the price, those wanting to sell have to drop it if they want to keep selling, and that is what happens on bar nine. On bar ten, the sellers try raising their prices again, but once again the buyers say "No!" The crowd's view of what is a fair price has not changed, and so they simply stop buying. The sellers are once again forced to lower their prices to keep selling, which we see happen on bars ten and eleven. On bars twelve and thirteen we see that the sellers make one final effort at pushing their price up. But the crowd view holds firm, and the buyers simply stop buying. Once again the sellers reduce their prices, and this time the price keeps on falling. By now the crowd may well have seen that they have the power to force the price back down. Those selling have tried — and failed — three times to raise their prices beyond this invisible ceiling. The crowd aren't dumb, they know that sooner or later the sellers will have to give up unless something happens in the meantime.

Now let's look at how that chart continues.

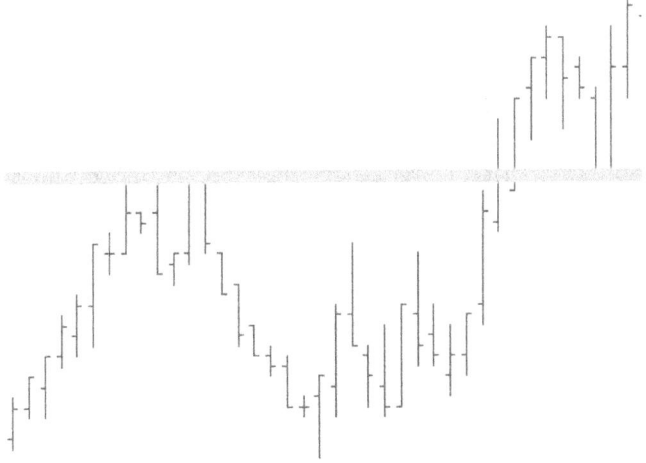

The price fell away, then there was a bit of backwards and forwards in opinion as it went up and down. About two thirds of the way along we see that the price rose quite sharply. It once again reached the invisible ceiling — the resistance — and for a short while the sellers were once again forced to drop their price. In the end though, the view of the crowd shifted, and enough became buyers to allow the price to continue to rise, breaking through the ceiling. Who knows what changed their minds? It could be there was some news, or it may be that more people believed the price would rise and so now was a good time to buy. What is important is what happened next.

The price broke through the invisible ceiling and carried on going up for a few bars. Then it dropped suddenly, and quickly returned to that invisible ceiling. But it didn't go any lower. Why not? One reason is that anyone in the crowd who wanted to buy at that price but missed out the first time around had a second chance. If they took that opportunity to buy, it meant more buyers in the market, which added weight to the view that the price would rise. Another reason is that it took a lot of buying for the price to break through the resistance ceiling. If anyone who bought at that point then sold at the same price or lower, they would take a loss on their investment. So the crowd included a large number of owners who had no desire to sell at that price. Fewer sellers makes for a rarer commodity, which means prices can rise.

Those are sound fundamental reasons the price can bounce off a previous resistance level. But there's another equally important reason: the self-fulfilling prophecy I mentioned before. A large proportion of people making up the market, the crowd, will be looking at the exact same chart. They will see the same things that we see. They will see the resistance, and they will see how the price broke through the resistance. And knowing that resistance often turns into *support*, they will interpret that as being a safe place to buy.

Trends

When price bars or candlesticks make continually higher highs and higher lows over a period of time, or they make continually lower highs and lower lows, we say that the price is trending. We can draw support or resistance lines on charts that are trending upwards or downwards, and we call these angled lines trend lines. Here is an example of an upwardly trending price, with a support trend line drawn in underneath.

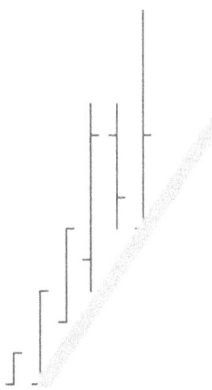

The *low* prices of the bars in this segment are, on average, rising with each bar. The high prices are also, on average, rising. When this happens, we say that the price is *trending upwards*. If we can connect several of these lows together with a straight line, as has been done in the example, we have a *trend line*. When the trend is upwards, this is effectively a form of support, and behaves just like the horizontal support line we saw earlier. The line can be drawn in as soon as there are enough bars to suggest its existence. There are no hard and fast rules about how many bars must be connected to make the trend line, but the more the better. The trend line, as with a regular horizontal support line, can be predictive. It gives us a hint that the price may well continue upwards. By extending the trend line beyond the end of the chart (as above), we can see the lowest prices that future bars are likely to make. As you might have figured out, a prediction like this can give us an opportunity to trade. We're looking for clues about where the price is headed next, and the trend line is suggesting it is upwards. If we were to buy while the price was close to the trend line, we would have a better than 50% chance of the price subsequently rising. Let's see how that chart continued:

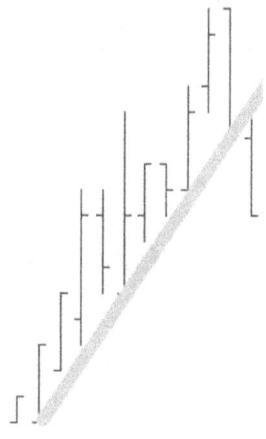

The price did continue upwards, bouncing off the trend line a couple more times. Eventually it dropped through. Before starting its descent though, as we can see from the final bar, it rose and touched the line before falling back. So just like with the horizontal resistance line becoming support, so this upwards support trend line became resistance after it was breached.

The reasons this up trend line works are exactly the same as the reasons a regular support line is effective. As the price rises, a number of traders will be looking to buy with a view to selling higher. When it falls back, this presents an opportunity to buy at a relatively good price. Those purchases cause the price to rise again, and an up trend is born. As more people see the trend and start drawing or imagining trend lines on their charts, an element of self-fulfilling prophecy comes into play and the line takes on a life of its own.

Patterns

Now we know how to find support, resistance, and trends on price charts, we can begin to look for patterns. We are going to look at two common patterns here.

TRIANGLES

Triangles occur when the price becomes constrained by a combination of two trend lines (one up and one down), or a trend line and either a horizontal support or a resistance line. Here's an example of the first variety:

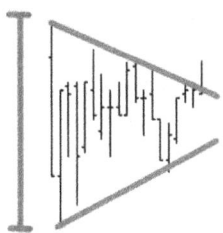

The price appears to be in a down trend (as shown by the down trend line) and an up trend, at the same time. This is a classic sign of indecision in the market. There is no consensus as to whether price is rising or falling. As time progresses, price becomes more and more constrained as there is more and more indecision. Two things could occur:

- This indecision continues, and the price keeps oscillating in a small range.

- A consensus view becomes predominant, and the price begins to rise or to fall.

In either case, the price will eventually break through one or both of the trend lines forming the triangle. If the price breaks out before it gets totally squeezed, then this is a strong sign consensus has been reached and the price is going to continue in the direction in which it broke through — as happened in the chart segment above. If on the other hand, the price breaks through the lines simply by virtue of the fact it is going sideways and there's no room left between the trend lines, then that suggests no consensus has yet been reached.

In the case of a consensus view and a break of the triangle (called a *breakout*), the triangle pattern itself provides a clue as to how far the price may continue in its new direction. The price difference between the low price and high price at the start of the triangle is roughly the distance the price is likely to travel. This is not a hard and fast rule, after all, nobody knows for sure what is going to happen. But it does occur frequently enough that we can say there is a higher probability of the price continuing that distance than it not doing so. Based on that probability, here is where we think the price has a fair chance of reaching in our example:

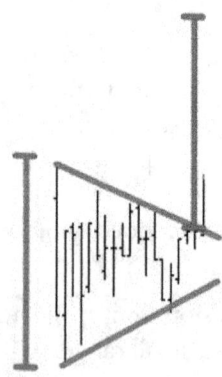

This is a possible buy signal. We know there is a good chance that the price is going to increase by the amount shown by the vertical line. Let's see what happened next:

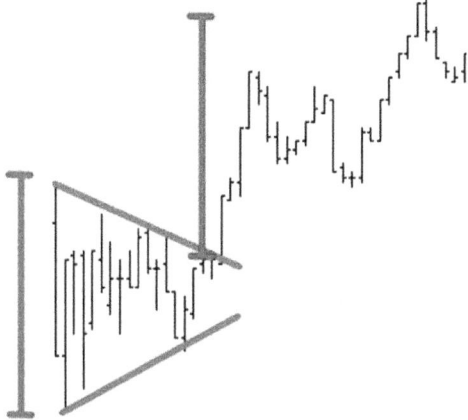

The price continued upwards, eventually reaching the level predicted by the triangle pattern. It didn't get there straight away, it fell short and even started to drop back, but it got there in the end. If we had bought at the moment the price broke out of the pattern, we could have sold at the target price suggested by the triangle for a healthy profit.

Consolidation

Triangle patterns always include at least one trend line, and may include a horizontal support or resistance line. Prices can also become constrained by two horizontal lines, one each of support and resistance. This is called a rectangle. Here is an example:

Here the price is constrained between a resistance and support. Near the end of the chart it suddenly pushes upwards, breaking out of the pattern and continuing its rise.

Consolidation patterns like this often occur after frantic periods of buying and selling. Participants in the market become wary of the recent price movement. Those who have been buying in an up trend for example, may wish to lock in some of their profit by selling their position. Enough selling will cause the price to drop. But the rise might not yet be over, and if enough people think it's going higher, they will push it back up. This can continue as buyers and sellers offload their positions and enter new positions, pushing the price up and down. All the mechanics of support and resistance are at work, just in close proximity. The price can either continue to drift sideways, or it will break out of the pattern. As with the triangle, the manner in which it effects its breakout gives us a clue as to where it is going next. If the price simply drifts outside the bounding lines, it isn't telling us much, there is no clear consensus. If on the other hand, the price pushes through one of the lines with force and determination — as is the case in the example above, where it moves strongly upwards in the space of a single bar — that's a sign there is a strong view on direction, and a good chance the price will continue to move in that direction.

Rectangle consolidation patterns provide the same signals and opportunities to us as their triangle cousins. By showing us the likely direction of the price, at least in the short term, we can make a decision as to whether we might want to buy or sell, whether we want to enter a new trade, or exit an existing one.

Indicators

Price bars and candlesticks show us a summary of price changes over time, and we can use different time scales to summarise those changes to a greater or lesser degree. We can go further though, by summarising price bars and candlesticks themselves. We do this by performing calculations on the values of bars and overlaying the results of those calculations on the chart. We call these overlaid calculations *indicators*. There are a whole raft of indicators, and it is beyond the scope of this book to explain each and every one. What is more important is to understand the principles behind them, and their uses.

Indicators can be useful in certain circumstances, but a lot of traders become too reliant on them, to the point where they forget their purpose, and even their meaning.

For the purposes of this overview, we will look at two basic types of indicator.

Moving Averages

A moving average is one of the most simple indicators that can be calculated on price. As its name would suggest, a moving average (often abbreviated to MA) is an average price value that moves with price.

The average price value is calculated over the previous n bars, where n is a number the trader decides upon. There are some common values for n, including 10, 21, 50, and 100. The lower the value, the faster the moving average reacts to changes in the price.

Although moving averages are very simple, there's a small complication in calculating them. We want to plot the average price over the last n bars, but each bar represents a range of prices, not a single price, so how do we choose which price in the range to use in the calculation? There are a number of options. We could add up the closing price of the last n bars and divide by n. Or we could add up the open price of the last n bars and divide that by n. Or we could use the high or low prices of the bars. A better way though, is to use the average price of each bar. We get that by adding together the high, low, and close of a bar and dividing the result by three (it's not a true average, it is slightly weighted towards the close price, but it is a common calculation). We make that calculation for each bar, we add the results together for the last n bars, then divide by n. The result is an average price over that n bar period, which we can plot on the chart when the nth bar closes.

It sounds more complicated than it is, and of course our charting software does all this work for us.

Here's what a 10 period moving average looks like on a bitcoin chart.

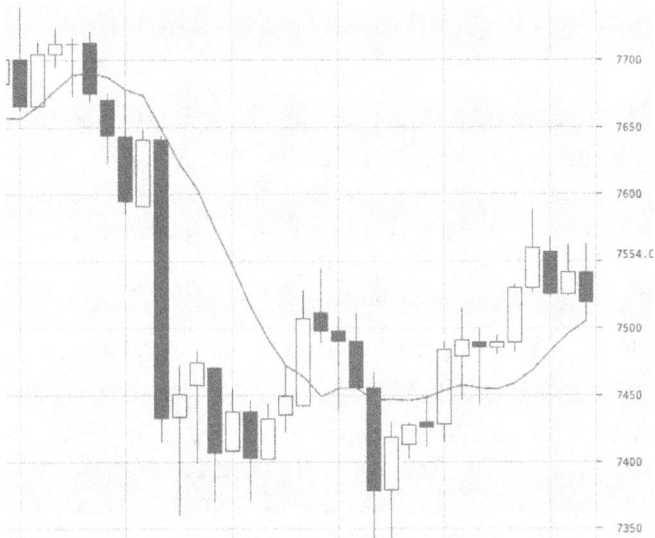

This is an example of a 10-period *simple* moving average, which we can abbreviate as *SMA(10)*. At any given candlestick, the line is showing us the average price over the last ten candlesticks.

There are variations to the moving average formula. The most common is to weight the formula to give more prominence to more recent bars. This is called an exponential moving average, or EMA, and the calculation is beyond the scope of this appendix. What's important is that an EMA reacts more quickly to changes in price.

Another variation is to include the volume of trades that took place in each candlestick in the calculation, so that candles where lots of trading took place are weighted more heavily than those where little trading took place. This is called a Volume Weighted Moving Average, or VWAP.

Moving averages form the basis of many simple trading strategies. They are useful in highlighting overall trends, for example.

Oscillators

Moving averages are plotted directly on a price chart, overlaying the price itself because they use the price scale. A different family of indicators called oscillators, use an entirely different scale, and are therefore plotted above or below the main price chart.

Oscillators are so called because their value oscillates, normally between two fixed values.

A common oscillator indicator is the Relative Strength Index, or RSI. The value of the RSI oscillates between values of 0 and 100. This indicator is all about measuring the momentum of price changes — which is to say the speed at which changes occur. The theory goes that if the RSI is above 70 or below 30, the price is considered to have extended too far too quickly, and is due a retracement or at least a pause.

As with moving averages, we can choose over how many prior price bars the RSI should be calculated; 14 is a very common value. We can also choose to change the default 30-70 oversold and overbought values to something else.

Oscillators like the RSI and the Commodity Channel Index (CCI) are sometimes referred to as leading indicators because they can provide signals that give an indication of future price direction. However, it is important to remember that they nothing more than calculations on price history, they are not magical!

Here's the RSI oscillator plotted on the previous chart example.

We can see that after the big price drop, as the RSI bounced off the lower 30-line ('oversold'), the price stopped falling and consolidated.

COMBINING INDICATORS

Traders who prefer to use indicators over reading pure price action, usually combine moving average-type indicators with an oscillator, using one to confirm signals generated by another. We look for the two types of indicator to be in agreement about the future direction of the price, putting the odds in our favour before entering a trade.

Appendix II - Sample Strategies

The purpose of this book is to introduce Bitcoin to experienced traders, not to teach the basics of trading or specific trading strategies. However, I'm fully aware that some people who read it will not have traded before. For those readers who are not traders, who have not already developed a profitable strategy they can adapt to the cryptocurrency market, this appendix introduces some sample trade setups to get you started.

I've included four setups here. That is not to say you should try to trade them all. Personally I use about three setups regularly, of which two make up more than eighty percent of all my trades. Knowing two setups inside out, being able to spot them and determine at a glance if a setup is worthy of a trade, is one of the keys to profitability. Too many beginner traders try to learn too many setups in their eagerness to have something to hand for every situation. It's tempting to try to have a setup for every situation, but patience truly is a virtue in the markets. The profitable trader knows precisely what they are looking for, waits patiently until they see it, then pounces.

What Is A Trading Strategy?

A trading strategy, or trading plan, is a formal methodology for trading a market. It defines everything about how we will trade. That means it designates the market and instrument(s) we are trading — in this case, bitcoin. It specifies how we will set up our charts (for example, we might choose 15 minute candlesticks with volume and a 10 period EMA). And most importantly it formalizes the setups we will trade. A setup is a price pattern, or a state of indicators, or a combination of both, that suggest we have a strong enough opinion of which direction the price is headed in to go ahead and enter a trade. Our strategy should also define how we exit a trade. We should always trade with a *stop loss* — an order that will exit our trade at the maximum loss we are willing to accept. As well as the stop loss, we should have a goal for where we are going to exit the trade if it becomes profitable. That goal will usually be integral to the setup.

Our trading strategy should be written down and strictly adhered to. There is no room in professional trading for gut instinct, or taking trades on a whim; that's called gambling. Which is not to say the strategy, once written, cannot be changed. Amendments, improvements, alterations, all are permitted over time, but they must always be tested and evaluated before being implemented.

Developing A Strategy

If you are new to trading, if you don't already have a profitable strategy, begin by reading through the setups presented here, pick one or two that click with you, and learn them thoroughly. Practice looking at old charts every day, trying to spot your chosen setups. Print charts out and draw on them. Mark entries and exits, see where the setups worked and where they didn't. Then move on to watching live charts. You will be amazed how much more difficult it is to spot a setup at the 'hard right edge' of a live chart than a fully developed old chart. Paper trade your chosen setups; that is, pretend-trade them. When you think you've seen a good trade entry, write down the exact time and the price you would be entering at if you were trading for real. Watch the trade play out as if you had really entered, and when you believe it is time to exit (whether at a profit or loss doesn't matter), write down the time together with your exit price. Keep practicing until your paper trades are profitable overall.

Being profitable overall does not mean winning more trades than we lose. We only need to win *bigger* than we lose. If we take ten trades, eight lose us $10 and two win us $100 each, we made $120 profit even though eighty percent of our trades were losers. This is what we mean by winning bigger than we lose.

The setups here are very commonly used and are well tried and tested. They are nothing Earth shattering, but they provide a starting point. If you feel you can tweak or adjust them, do so. Test your new and improved version by paper trading it. Every trader is unique and will bring something to the way they interpret and implement a strategy.

Setup Types

Broadly speaking we can subdivide technical trading setups into two sets of two categories:

- Trend-following
- Counter-trend

And:

- Price-based
- Indicator-based

Trend-following setups are those where we trade in the same direction as the overall trend. Take the following chart:

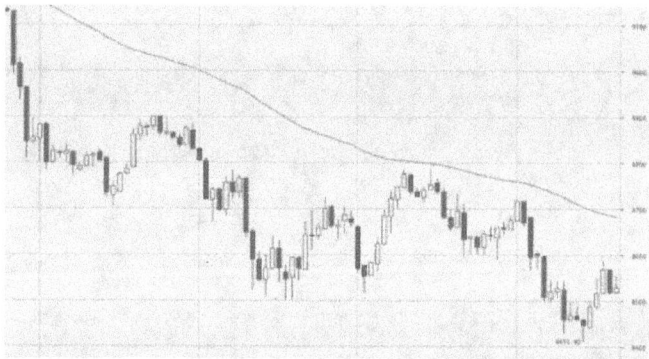

The general trend here is down, as highlighted by the moving average. Trend following setups then, would look to go short. Counter-trend setups would be looking for the end of the trend and a change of direction.

As the old saying goes, a rising tide lifts all boats. Trading in the same direction as the general trend, i.e. going with the tide, is lower risk than trying to find the end of a trend (or trying to pinpoint the exact moment the tide turns). By definition, the end of a trend occupies less space on the chart than the trend itself; we have a greater chance of taking a bite out of the trend than we do of nailing the moment it switches. For beginner traders I recommend only trying to trade in the direction of the trend.

That leaves us with a choice of whether to use indicators on our charts. Personally I prefer pure price action. Almost every indicator is a calculation based on past prices (some are calculated on volume), so those indicators are providing a summary of information already on the chart. Summaries can be useful, but if we learn to read the price itself, there is no need for indicators. As I said earlier, every trader is unique, and plenty swear by their indicators, so I have included an indicator based strategy as well as some of my preferred price-only setups.

Setup 1: Triangle

This is one of the most basic price action patterns, one of the easiest to spot, and is among the most successful. In trading, simple is good. Triangles occur often, they give us clear entry signals, an idea of where to exit if the trade does not work out, and a good price target at which to take profit if it does.

We already looked at triangles in Appendix I, so let's take a look at a winning bitcoin trade based on a triangle setup. This is a five minute BTC/USD chart.

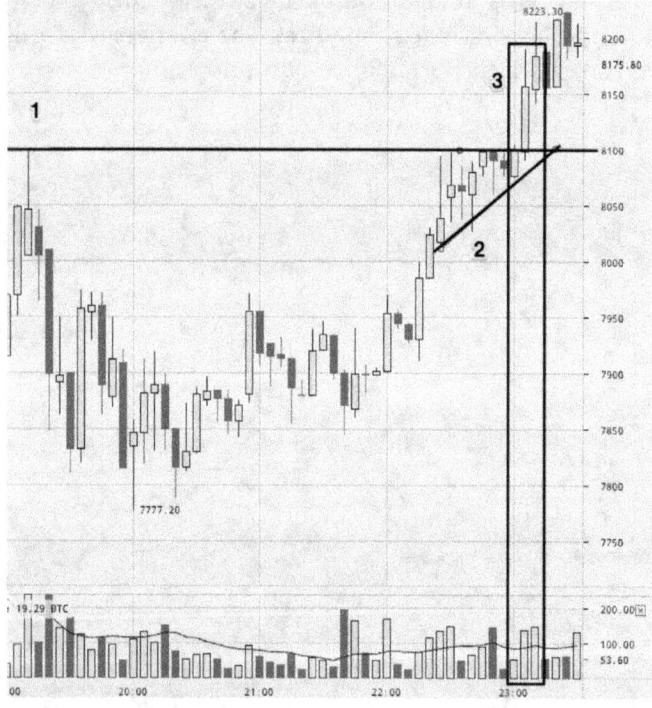

- The price is moving generally upwards in the second half of the chart, so we are favouring going long (buying bitcoin with US dollars, to sell the bitcoin back at a higher price).

• The price begins to meet resistance as marked by the horizontal line. Note that this line is a previous high (shown at figure 1) and also a double-zero round number, making it significant.

• Although the highs of the candlesticks get stuck at the resistance, the lows continue to get higher, and the triangle pattern forms.

• At figure 3, when the price breaks out of the top, we see the volume is increasing. This is a sign of momentum behind the move. The breakout on growing volume is our signal to enter the trade.

• We would place a stop loss order below the uptrend line forming the bottom of the triangle — if the price reached there the pattern would have failed and we would exit for a small loss of about $25 per bitcoin traded.

• Our target for exit is given by the mouth of the triangle, which is about $100 per bitcoin (8000-8100). Compared to a possible loss of $25, we have a risk:reward ratio of 4:1 (i.e. we stand to win four times as much as we stand to lose).

• As we can see, the price easily achieved the target, moving a bit more than $100 in our favour.

Summary: Triangles are about as simple as it gets, and they work. It is entirely possible to make a good living trading only triangles in the direction of the trend.

Setup 2: Inside Bar

An inside bar is a candlestick which occurs within the range of the previous candlestick. In a sideways market it carries little meaning, but in a trend it is a sign of consolidation. If we zoomed in on an inside bar pattern, going from a ten minute chart to a one minute for example, the inside bar would probably show a triangle pattern. Here's what the inside bar pattern looks like:

The second bar is an inside bar because it occurs completely within the range of the preceding bar. An inside bar can be the same colour as the preceding bar, or the opposite colour, it doesn't really matter. Some traders only count a bar as being a valid inside bar if it occurs within the body of the previous bar (i.e. within the open and close prices).

We can use this setup as either trend-following, showing us the continuation of a trend, or as a counter trend strategy, showing us a possible change of direction. Here we are going to define the inside bar setup as only being valid *in the direction of the trend*, because we have a higher probability of success when we go with the flow of the market.

To trade an inside bar setup:

- The inside bar must occur within a trend.
- Once we see an inside bar form, we look for the next bar to break out above or below the high or

low of the inside bar, in the direction of the trend. Such a break is a valid entry signal.

• A more lenient version of this strategy allows entry on any bar after the inside bar. Again, we want the odds stacked in our favour as much as possible, so we are using the stricter definition of a valid entry; it must occur on the bar immediately after the inside bar, otherwise no trade.

• We place a stop loss order on the opposite side of the inside bar. In other words if the trade is long, we put a stop just below the low of the inside bar. If it's short, place it just above the high.

• Unlike a triangle, this pattern does not predict an exit. Our price target should be based on the conditions and any strong areas of support and resistance. Failing that, we can use a *trailing stop* — a stop loss order that we move as the trade goes in our favour. Trailing stops should be ratcheted, that is, as the price goes our way we move the stop by the same amount, but if the price comes back against us, we do not move the stop back again.

Here's a chart segment with several inside bar patterns.

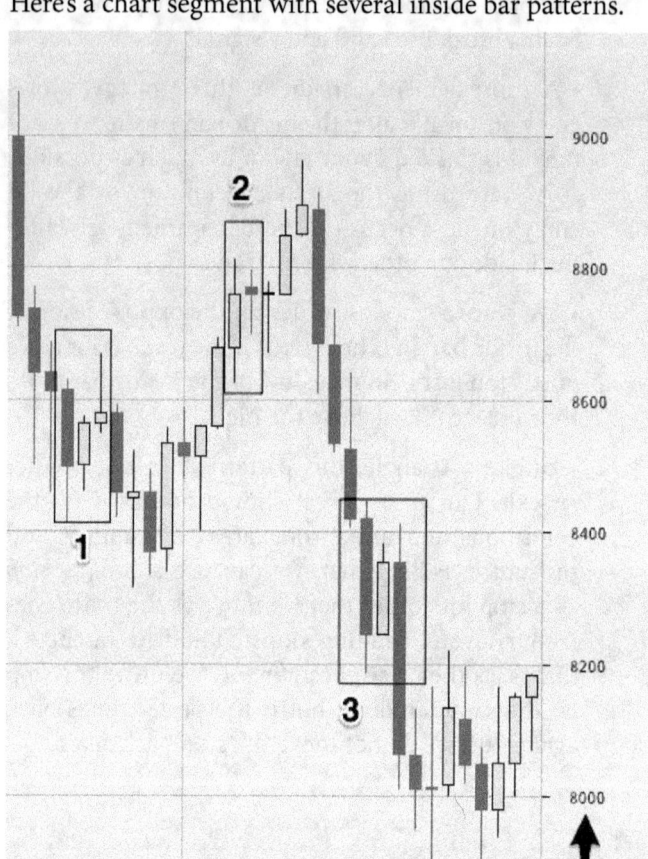

The first pattern occurs in box 1, but we'll come back to that one.

In box 2 we have a trade opportunity. The price has been moving strongly in one direction (up) and has paused, creating an inside bar (the filled bar in box 2). We would look to enter a long trade (buying BTC with US dollars, to sell it back at a higher price for a profit) if on the next bar the price exceeds the high of the previous bar, which is a little over 8800. Our stop would be just below the low of the first bar in box 3 — around 8600. Here are the entry and stop marked on the chart:

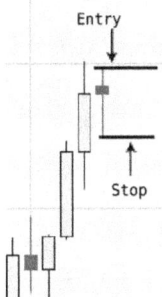

The next bar failed to break above the entry price, so this pattern failed and there was no trade. Note that if we were trading the less strict version of the pattern, the second bar after the inside bar did break out above and would have got us in for a small win.

In box 3 we see an inside bar as the price consolidates in a strong downward move, so we would look to go short (selling bitcoin for US dollars, to buy it back at a lower price, the difference being our profit) if the price broke below the low of the previous bar. Here's what that looks like:

As we can see on the main chart, the price broke below the entry level on the next bar, so we would enter a trade.

A sensible price target would be the triple zero round number of 8000. The price reached this target very quickly, and bounced around there for a fair time before retracing, giving us plenty of time to get out with a profit of around $200 per bitcoin traded.

Notice there is is another inside bar that occurred after this trade ended, but as the price had started going sideways there was no clear trend and this was therefore not a valid setup.

Now let's go back to box 1. The bar following the inside bar did not break our entry signal, so under our strict rules there was no trade here. However, that bar happens to be a special pattern of its own called a *pin bar*. A pin bar is usually defined as a bar where the body makes up less than a quarter of the total height of the bar, and is a sign that the price has tried to move in one direction, but has failed and come back to almost where it started. When a pin bar immediately follows an inside bar, as we see in box 1, it's a strong signal that the original trend is about to resume. Therefore it would have been a valid trade to go short on the break below the inside bar on the bar immediately following the pin bar.

Box 1 is an example of why learning to read the price can open up new and interesting trading opportunities. A fixed strategy based on strict indicators is inflexible and leaves a lot of money on the table. When we learn to read price, we can begin by trading similarly strict rules, but with experience we can read additional signals — like the pin bar — and combine them with our rules to come up with trades we would otherwise have missed.

Setup 3: Second Wind

Often when the price moves a relatively large distance, quickly, it will take a moment to consolidate before getting a 'second wind' and continuing its trajectory, moving the same distance again. If we are to attempt to trade some of that second move, we need a sign that it is about to happen and that we have not simply shifted into a sideways phase of the market. The sign we use is volume. Here are the entry criteria for entering a second wind setup.

- The price must have moved strongly and quickly for at least three bars in the same direction, and on increasing volume. This indicates strong momentum in the move.

- When it retraces or goes sideways, those bars should be on lower volume, showing there is little momentum in the opposite direction. At this point we prepare to enter a trade if the price breaks below the previous low.

Our price target for the trade is a move of equivalent distance to the initial part of the move. We can also exit if we see a bar against us on increased volume, indicating momentum has shifted.

Here's an example of a winning Second Wind trade setup. This is a five minute BTC/USD chart.

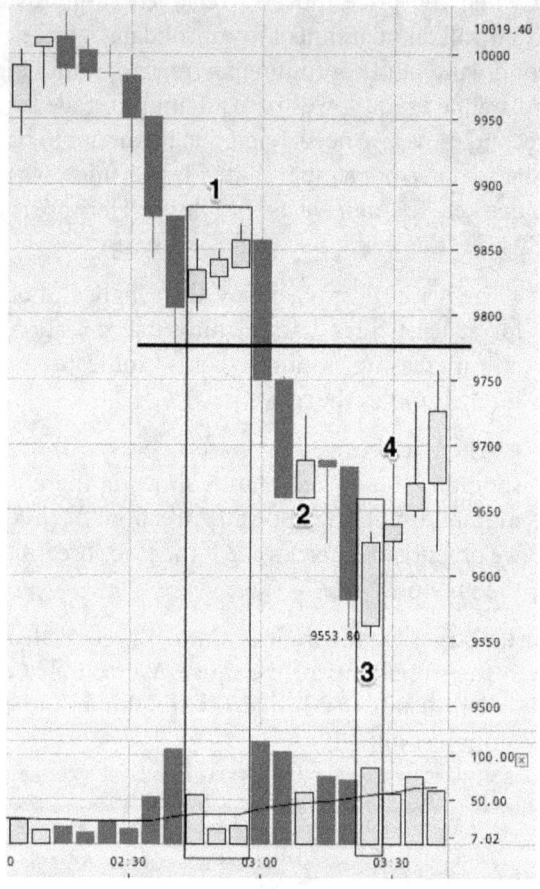

- The move begins slowly as the price drops away from 10,000, and as the price drops faster the volume increases. This high-momentum drop is the first sign there might be a trade here.

- In box 1 the price pauses to consolidate. Note we see an inside bar form at the start of the box. The next bar does not break below the inside bar, rendering that particular setup void. However, as the consolidation continues the volume drops away. This is now a valid Second Wind setup, and we prepare to enter a short trade (selling bitcoin) if and when the price breaks below the previous low, shown by the horizontal line around 9775.

- The price does indeed break that low, so we enter our short trade. We are expecting the price to drop quickly (because we believe this to be the second half of a larger overall drop), so we can place our stop loss quite tightly. A good position would be just above the 9,800 double zero round number. If the stop order is hit, our loss will be about $25. Our target exit is the same distance the price dropped originally, which was about $225 (from 10,000 to 9,775). That gives us a price target of 9,550. Our risk:reward ratio for this trade is $25:$225, which is a very healthy 9:1.

- At figure 2 the price consolidates again. However, as it does so on reduced volume, there is no reason to exit the trade. Note that this is another inside bar setup, which further adds to our opinion that the price will drop more. If we were the conservative sort, we could exit half of our position here to lock in some profit.

- The price almost hits the 9,550 target, getting within $3 before bouncing. This would be the perfect time to exit, netting a profit of at least $200 per bitcoin traded. If we used our alternative exit and waited for a bar against us on higher volume, we would exit our trade either at the bar marked 3, when the volume exceeded that of the previous bar, or at the open of the bar at figure 4. Either way, we would still net well over $100 per bitcoin.

The Second Wind trade gives us an alternative way into big, fast moves. The different options for exiting mean it can be tailored to suit the trader and their tolerance for risk.

Setup 4: Simple MA Cross + MFI

This is another super-simple setup, and this time we're using indicators to show us the way. We are looking for a fast moving average to cross below a slower one to give us an entry. That's a bit too simple though! If we traded every moving average cross that came our way, we would be whipped about and die a death of a thousand cuts. We need to filter the crosses so we take only those with the best chance of success. We use two filters. The first is an even longer moving average, and the second is an indicator called the Money Flow Index, or MFI.

The MFI is an *oscillator* that uses price and volume to measure buy and sell pressure. Usually it is used like the RSI to highlight overbought or oversold signals, but we're using it as a momentum indicator here.

Our trade setup is as follows:

> • Onto our chart we place three moving averages. Because we are trading bitcoin and are therefore in a market dominated by unsophisticated traders (in the nicest possible way), we stick to the default settings so we are seeing what the crowd is seeing. On Cryptowat.ch, the defaults for the EMA are 10, 21, and 100 periods. We also add the MFI indicator, but as we are using it in a non-standard way as a filter and not the primary signal, we change it to a 2 period setting.

> • We only want to trade in the same direction as the overall trend. To determine that trend, we want the price and the two faster EMAs to all be

on the same side of the EMA(100). So if the price and the EMA(10) and EMA(21) are all above the EMA(100), we look to go long, if they are all below it, we look to go short. And if they are split above and below, there are no trades.

• Our entry signal is as follows: the EMA(10) must cross the EMA(21) in the direction in which we want to trade. At the same time, the MFI must be 100 (for a long trade) or 0 (for a short trade).

• We exit either when the EMA(10) crosses back over the EMA(21), or when a bar closes on the wrong side of the EMA(10), whichever occurs first.

Here's an example.

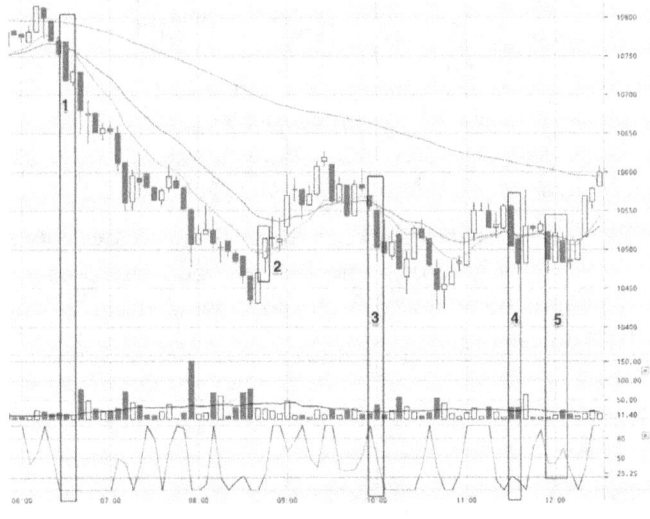

• The slowest EMA (the 100 period) is the line at the top. At the start of this chart, although the other two EMAs are below the EMA(100), the price is above it, so there are no trades possible.

• By the time we reach box 1, the price is also below the EMA(100), so we are prepared to take short trades. In other words, we will be looking to sell bitcoin for US dollars with a view to buying the bitcoin back at a lower price, the difference being our profit.

• In box 1, the EMA(10) crosses below the EMA(21). This is our primary entry signal. Because the MFI is at 0, our entry is confirmed. We go short at about 10,725. We could place our stop loss order above the high of the previous bar, or above the nearest round number.

• When a candlestick closes above the EMA(10) in box 2, we have our signal to exit. That happens at around 10,525, netting us a profit of $200 per BTC.

• In box 3, there is another cross of the EMA(10) below the EMA(21). However, the MFI is not at 0, so we do not enter.

• Boxes 4 and 5 are the same — the MFI keeps us out of these low-momentum moves, which as we can see, would not have been profitable.

• By the end of the chart the price has crossed above the EMA(100), so no further trades are possible until the price and faster EMAs are all in agreement once more.

Summary

We have looked at three pure price setups and one indicator-based setup. These give a flavour of the sorts of rules that should go into a trading strategy. I reiterate that these setups are presented purely as a starting point for your own strategy. I have traded bitcoin using all of them successfully, but every trader is unique and should choose and adapt setups that match their trading style.

When creating your own strategy, I urge you to favour simplicity. Modern charting packages offer a plethora of fancy indicators and it is tempting to slap loads of them onto a chart in an effort to weed out losing trades. It feels logical that the more indicators we have, the better the signal when they all line up and say "Buy!" But adding complication is unnecessary. It increases stress and creates too much opportunity for error. It is important to remember the market is made of people, and that the chart shows us what the people are doing. No magic combination of indicators can ever predict with great accuracy what they will do next.

All we need if we are to make money, is to make bigger winning trades than losing ones. A slight edge, repeated, is enough to generate consistent profits, and simple reading of price, simple recognition of patterns that work time and again, is a great edge.

Glossary

Air-Gapped

An air-gapped machine is one not connected to the internet. Pre-wifi ,the name made more sense because it referred to the empty air between the network port on the wall and the machine. Air-gapping is a security measure designed to ensure no malware can enter a machine.

Altcoin

A name given to any digital token that isn't Bitcoin. (Abbreviation of 'alternative coin').

Asymmetric Cryptography

See: Public key cryptography.

Bag Holder

The victim left holding a commodity at a loss after those on the inside of a *pump and dump* scam have dumped their holdings, causing the price to drop.

BIP

Bitcoin Improvement Proposal. A technical document in which improvements to Bitcoin are suggested in detail. As there is no central authority overseeing Bitcoin, it's usually up to wallet creators and/or exchanges to adopt improvements as they see fit.

Bitcoin

The first decentralised digital currency. Created by *Satoshi Nakamoto* and released in January 2009. Based on *blockchain* technology to secure an open ledger allowing for peer-to-peer transactions.

Bitcoin Cash

A cryptocurrency resulting from a *fork* of Bitcoin on 1st August 2017.

Block

A single unit within the *blockchain*. A block contains a list of *confirmed* transactions.

Blockchain

An open, distributed ledger consisting of an ever-growing set of records which are linked and secured cryptographically, making them effectively immutable.

Brain Wallet

Literally a wallet that is held inside someone's brain. Usually just the private key will be memorised, with the Bitcoin address itself being written down somewhere, but it's quite possible to memorise the whole thing. Alternatively a BIP39 seed mnemonic can be memorised, and can be used subsequently to recreate the wallet in a suitable app.

Breakout

In trading terminology, a breakout occurs when the price breaks above or below a *support* or *resistance* level, usually on increased volume.

Brute Force Attack

A way of defeating cryptography or password protection by trying every possible combination of letters, numbers, and symbols to discover a password or key. The longer the password, the exponentially longer it takes to brute force it.

Cash Out

Exchange cryptocurrency for fiat currency.

Change

In Bitcoin, change is the part of an *Unspent Transaction Output* (UTXO) that is sent back to the wallet originating a transaction, in order to not spend the entire UTXO. Change is a necessary function of Bitcoin because the protocol does not allow the spending of fractions of a UTXO.

Cold Storage

Any form of Bitcoin storage where the private key is not connected to the internet. Paper wallets are a common form of cold storage.

Confirmation (Confirmed)

A transaction receives confirmation it has been added to the blockchain once it has been included in a mined block. As more blocks are added to the chain, the transaction is said to receive further confirmations. For example, if a transaction is confirmed in a block and three more blocks have been added to the chain since then, the transaction has four confirmations. The more confirmations a transaction has, the harder it is to alter, as every block after the one the transaction is in would have to be re-mined.

Cryptocurrency (Also: Crypto)

A digital currency secured by cryptography, usually based on *blockchain* technology.

Digital Signature

The cryptographic encoding of data with a *private key* such that it can only be decrypted with the corresponding *public key*, thus proving the provenance of the data. In Bitcoin, a transaction is digitally signed with the *private key* associated with the sending address, thus proving that the originator of the transaction has control over that address.

Digital Token

Another term commonly used to refer to cryptocurrencies like Bitcoin.

Double Spending

Spending the same bitcoin more than once. The blockchain at the heart of Bitcoin means double spending is impossible. However, that doesn't mean people can't or don't try. Sometimes this happens inadvertently, for example, if the same software wallet is copied to two separate devices, they may not always be perfectly synchronised with the blockchain at any given moment and therefore if a transaction is sent from one and another transaction is immediately sent from the other, they will try to send the same coin. The first transaction to confirm will then prevent the second from confirming and it will fail. Sometimes people deliberately try to double spend bitcoin for their own financial advantage. This is why, if you are selling goods or services, it is advisable to always wait for multiple *confirmations* before considering a transaction to be valid.

Ethereum

Not a cryptocurrency as such, Ethereum describes itself as a blockchain-based distributed computing platform and operating system featuring *smart contracts*. We can think of it as being a sort of toolkit for building cryptocurrencies and applications that use them.

Exchange

A place where cryptocurrency can be bought or sold. The exchange may buy and sell directly to customers, or match customer orders enabling trade, or both.

Fee

An amount of bitcoin sent with every transaction. The fee is awarded to the *miner* who *confirms* the transaction. A higher fee will usually result in a transaction being mined more quickly.

Fiat (Currency)

Government or state-backed currency that has been established and accepted as money, despite having no intrinsic value, i.e. not being backed by anything of value (such as gold). US dollars, euros, and pounds are all fiat currencies.

Fork

In computing terms, a fork is a copy of a software project that deviates from the original. Because cryptocurrency is software, it too can be forked. Bitcoin is constantly evolving, but the core developers who maintain it do not always agree on how it should move forwards. That can lead to factions breaking off and going in one direction while the remainder go in another. *Bitcoin Cash* was a fork of Bitcoin that occurred on 1st August 2017.

Fractional Reserve Banking

The system of banking prevalent in the western world. Commercial banks are required to only hold a fraction of customer deposits in reserve, and can lend out the rest as loans. This process creates new money, as loaned money is spent, banked, and re-loaned.

Hash (Algorithm)

An algorithm that takes any piece of data, performs a calculation upon it, and returns a unique value of a fixed length called a *hash value*. If a hash value is published alongside a block of data, anyone accessing that data can check it has not been changed by running the hash algorithm themselves and comparing their result with the published value. If they match, the data was identical at the time the algorithm was run. In Bitcoin, a hash algorithm is calculated on all data comprising a *block*. If anything in the block is changed, the hash algorithm will output a different value. Thus it becomes possible for anyone participating in the Bitcoin network to verify instantly that a block has not been tampered with.

Hash Value

The result of a hash algorithm.

Hierarchical Deterministic (HD) Wallet

A wallet conforming to the BIP32 proposal. HD wallets use a seed value from which all subsequent addresses and their associated *private keys* are derived. If the seed value is known, the same addresses can be recreated. This makes it easier to back up, move, or re-create a wallet as only the seed value must be known. On the other hand, if the seed value falls into the wrong hands, the entire wallet is compromised.

ICO (Initial Coin Offering)

The selling of pre-mined tokens of a new cryptocurrency before that currency becomes publicly traded on any exchanges. Most ICOs are actually scams, and the currency sold has no value. Avoid.

Indicator

A calculation performed on price and / or volume data and either overlaid on a price chart or plotted alongside it to summarise that data in a meaningful way. Common indicators include moving averages, RSI, and stochastics.

Limit (Order)

An order to buy or sell at a specified price or better. Limit orders are what can be seen when looking at the *order book*.

Litecoin

A popular cryptocurrency released in 2011. Litecoin aims to process blocks approximately four times faster than Bitcoin.

Mempool

Short for memory pool, the mempool is the list of transactions waiting to be picked up by a *miner* in their next block.

Miner

An entity performing the *mining* operation which simultaneously *confirms* transactions and creates new bitcoins.

Mining

The process of confirming transactions through *proof-of-work*. The result of mining is both confirmed blocks added to the *blockchain*, and new bitcoins created. Once 21 million bitcoins have been created, the mining process will only confirm transaction blocks.

Monero

Another popular cryptocurrency, released in 2014. Monero prioritises privacy, and unlike Bitcoin it obscures the sender, recipient, and amount in every transaction, making transactions impossible to follow with a blockchain explorer. Monero is often used as a middle-man to obscure the source of bitcoin (i.e. to launder it). By buying monero with bitcoin, then buying back bitcoin with monero, the bitcoin transaction chain is broken and the original source of funds can never been known with 100% certainty.

Node

A machine running Bitcoin client software that can receive broadcast transactions and send them on to other nodes, until they are picked up by a *miner*.

Nonce

A random value added to a block of transactions before the *hash algorithm* is run against the combined data. Because only *hash values* starting with lots of zeros are considered valid, it is necessary to try recalculating the hash with a lot (billions) of different nonce values until one is found that gives an acceptable output. This is a computationally expensive task (requiring considerable computing resources and electricity).

Order Book
A list of Limit orders that have not yet been fulfilled.

Oscillator
An *indicator* whose value oscillates within a predetermined range. An oscillator is usually plotted below a price chart rather than overlaid on it because its scale is unrelated to the price scale. RSI and CCI are two very common oscillators.

Peer-to-Peer Network
A computing network without a central server or hub. Bitcoin is a peer-to-peer network.

Pin Bar
A bar or candlestick in which the real body occupies less than a quarter of the range of the bar, and in which the real body is at either the top or bottom of the bar. A pin bar shows that during the time period the bar covers, the price has been pushed in one direction but ultimately has recovered almost to where it was at the start of the period. Depending on where a pin bar occurs and the form it takes, it can either suggest the continuation of a trend after consolidation, or the reversal of one.

Private Key
In cryptography, a private key is a sequence of characters and digits that can be used to decrypt information that has been encrypted with an associated *public key*, and encrypt information that can then be decrypted with the associated public key. A private key should never be shared. In Bitcoin, the private key is used to *digitally sign* transactions, proving their provenance. Every Bitcoin address has

an associated private key, and whoever is in possession of that key can spend the funds in the wallet.

Proof of Work

A task that is very difficult to perform, but very easy to verify has been done once completed. Bitcoin mining is a proof of work task. Proof of work is required to add a block to the blockchain. By making this task computationally (and therefore financially) expensive, it becomes uneconomical (and after a while, computationally impossible) to manipulate data in the blockchain retroactively. The proof of work requirement is what makes the blockchain immutable.

Public Key

A sequence of characters and numbers that can be used to encrypt data which can be later be decrypted with the associated *private key*, and can be used to decrypt data that was encrypted with the associated private key. A public key can be freely shared. In Bitcoin, a public key associated with a Bitcoin address can be used to verify the *digital signature* attached to a transaction from that address, thus confirming that the transaction was authorised by the holder of the private key.

Public Key Cryptography

A system of cryptography in which the keys for encrypting and decrypting information are different. These keys are mathematically related. Because they are different, one (the *public key*) can be freely shared with all parties who wish to send encrypted data, or who wish to read the *digital signature* attached to a piece of data. Bitcoin uses public key cryptography to secure wallets and transactions.

Pump & Dump

An insider trading scam in which the organiser buys a (usually) thinly traded commodity then encourages others to do so, thus pushing up the price. As the price rises, they sell their holding to these new buyers, realising an almost guaranteed profit. Eventually as more people begin to sell their holding, the price collapses, leaving *bag holders* who now own a commodity they can only sell at a loss. Because less-popular cryptocurrencies trade very little volume, they are relatively easy to manipulate and are therefore prime targets for pump & dump scams.

Resistance

A level above which price has failed to rise on at least two recent occasions.

Satoshi

The smallest unit of bitcoin. A single bitcoin is divided into one hundred million satoshi. Therefore 1 satoshi = 0.00000001 BTC.

Satoshi Nakamoto

The unknown person or group of people who created Bitcoin.

Smart Contract

Computer code that runs within a digital currency, giving the currency added functionality.

Stop (Loss)

An order to buy or sell at a specified price or worse. A stop loss order is entered once in a position, to exit that position if the price goes the 'wrong' way.

Support

A level below which price has failed to fall on at least two recent occasions.

Sweeping A Wallet

Transferring the entire contents of one wallet into another.

Trailing Stop

A stop order that moves as a trade goes into profit. Trailing stops usually ratchet, moving only in one direction, locking in profits. Some trading platforms can trail stop orders automatically.

Trend

A period during which prices are generally rising or falling.

Trend Line

A support or resistance line drawn on a chart, connecting multiple highs or lows.

Unspent Transaction Output (UTXO)

A bitcoin transaction that has been received to a wallet and not yet spent.

Wallet

A medium for storing a Bitcoin address and its associated keys, and optionally for originating and receiving transactions.

Warm (or Hot) Storage

A wallet which is connected to the internet and can therefore communicate with the Bitcoin network.

Also by Harvey Walsh

www.ingramcontent.com/pod-product-compliance
Lightning Source LLC
Chambersburg PA
CBHW052313220526
45472CB00001B/104